Prestel Muse

Technisches Museum Wien

Prestel
Munich · Berlin · London · New York

Editor: Gabriele Zuna-Kratky

Second revised and enlarged edition
© 2005 – Technisches Museum Wien and
Prestel Verlag, Munich · Berlin · London ·
New York

Front cover: Technisches Museum Wien
Back cover: Haswell's forging press

Photo credits:
All photographs Peter Sedlaczek, Technisches Museum Wien or the archive of Technisches Museum Wien, except: Foto Donhauser 28, 29, 32, 33, 34, 40, 142, 151; VA Erzberg GmbH 53; Österreichisches Institut für Zeitgeschichte – Vienna, Bildarchiv 65; VEÖ/Graf 83, 85; Österreichisches Gesellschafts- und Wirtschaftsmuseum 105, Martin Müller 98, 99, 101; Siemens-Forum 112; Deutsches Museum, Munich 168; Hertha Hurnaus 172; Peter Levenitschnig 190.

Texts by:
Zita Breu (BrZ), Peter Donhauser (DoP), Mechthild Dubbi (DuM), Manuela Fellner-Feldhaus (FeM), Barbara Hafok (HaA), Beatrix Hain (HaB), Reinhard Keimel (KeR), Karl Heinz Knauer (KnK), Helmut Lackner (LaH), Otmar Moritsch (MoO), Lisa Noggler (NoL), Wolfgang Pensold (PeW), Gerhard Schaukal (ScG), Hannelore Stöckl (StH), Walter Szevera (SzW), Manfred Tragner (TrM), Gabriele Zuna-Kratky

Subeditors: Barbara Pilz, Helmut Lackner

Deutsche Bibliothek holds a record of this publication in the Deutsche Nationalbibliografie; detailled bibliographical data can be found at: http://dnb.ddb.de

Prestel Verlag
Königinstraße 9 · 80539 Munich
Tel. +49 (89) 38 17 09-0
Fax +49 (89) 38 17 09-35

Prestel Publishing Ltd.
4 Bloomsbury Place · London WC1A 2QA
Tel. +44 (29) 73 23-5004
Fax +44 (20) 76 36-8004

Prestel Publishing
900 Broadway, Suite 603
New York, NY 10003
Tel. +1 (212) 995-2720
Fax +1 (212) 995-2733

www.prestel.com

Information

Technisches Museum Wien
Mariahilfer Str. 212 · 1140 Wien
Tel. +43 (1) 8 99 98-60 00
Fax +43 (1) 8 99 98-11 11
E-Mail: mbox@tmw.at
www.technischesmuseum.at

The museum's reading room is open to the public.

Österreichische Mediathek
Publikumsbetrieb Marchettischlössl
Gumpendorfer Straße 95 · 1060 Wien
Tel. +43 (1) 5 97 36 69-20
Fax +43 (1) 5 97 36 69-25
www.mediathek.at

Leitung, Technik, Archiv
Webgasse 2a · 1060 Wien
Tel. +43 (1) 5 97 36 69-0
Fax +43 (1) 5 97 36 69-40

Translated from the German by Stephen Telfer, Edinburgh, and Brad Steiner, Berlin (pp. 98–117)

Layout and production by Rainald Schwarz, Munich
Copy-edited by Claudia Hellmann and Delius Producing Munich
Printing and binding: Passavia, Passau

Printed in Germany on acid-free paper

ISBN 3-7913-3518-9 (English edition)
ISBN 3-7913-3519-7 (German edition)

Index

Foreword 4
On the Museum's History 6

The Collection 14
Images of Technology 18
Nature and Knowledge 26
Heavy Industry 46
Energy 66
Mass Production – Luxury Goods 86
Everyday Life – Directions for Use 98
medien.welten 118
Musical Instruments 136
Transport 152
The 'Mini' 172

Education at the Technisches Museum Wien 174
Archive and Library 178
The Conservation Section 186
Depots 188
Österreichische Mediathek:
The Austrian Multimedia Centre 190

Foreword

Since re-opening in 1999, the Technisches Museum Wien has been re-energized in its mission to explain the fundamental principles of technology and its developments. It is an exciting, hands-on museum that addresses current issues in science and technology.

The Museum's rich heritage and collections allow it to juxtapose the old and the new. Employing the latest museum techniques, it makes historical objects accessible to today's visitors. This means, for instance, that visitors will find 19th century models alongside hands-on exhibits. The Technisches Museum Wien works continually to develop what it has to offer young and old alike – guided tours, education programmes and 'camp ins', for instance. The 'Mini' is an activities' area designed specially for our young visitors between the ages of two and six.

To get to where the Museum is today, a huge amount of work was necessary. Before its collections could be re-arranged, the building had to be refurbished. Among the exhibitions that have now re-opened are 'Nature and Knowledge', 'Images of Technology', 'Heavy Industry', 'Energy', 'Mass Production – Luxury Goods', which looks at technology and design from the Biedermeier era until 1873, 'Musical Instruments', a special feature on 'Transport', 'medien.welten', which looks at information and communication, and 'Everyday Life – Directions for Use', which looks at technology in everyday life. Since 2001, a part of Austria's audiovisual memory has been housed in the Technisches Museum in the form of the Österreichische Mediathek, a multimedia centre.

Besides exhibiting objects, the Museum also collects and conserves them. Its Archive and Library play just as important a role in these activities as its Depots and Conservation Section. All in all, the Technisches Museum Wien is in a process of continuous change.

As the third largest museum of science and technology in Europe and the only one in Austria with a comprehensive remit, the Technisches Museum Wien takes education seriously. Its staff looks forward to welcoming you on your next visit to their permanent and temporary exhibitions.

Gabriele Zuna-Kratky and
the staff at the Technisches Museum Wien

On the Museum's History

First page of the document calling for the establishment of a Technical Museum of Trade and Industry in Vienna, c. 1909. Print

Technological Collections: the Museum's Forerunners

The basis of the collections now held by the museum is formed by a collection established by imperial decree on 11 September 1807. The 'Fabriksprodukten-Kabinett' (Collection of Manufactured Products) was to be a collection of 'exemplars of manufactured articles' that provided an overview of the degree of perfection of the products of the 'useful arts' and their gradual development. The collection was intended to illustrate the levels attained by Austrian manufacturing industry of the day. The collection was at first provisionally housed in a private home and, in 1815 together with the 'Physikalisch-astronomisches Kabinett' (Physical and Astronomical Collection) founded by Emperor Franz I, was incorporated into the Polytechnical Institute, the forerunner of the current Vienna University of Technology. The Polytechnical Institute's constitution as drafted by Johann Joseph Prechtl in 1817 stated that the Institute saw itself not only as a technical school, but also, for the first time, that it viewed itself as a Technological Museum, or 'Konservatorium für Künste und Gewerbe' (Conservatory for the Arts and Industry), and as a 'Verein zur Beförderung der Nationalindustrie' (Association for the Promotion of Austrian Industry). Its technical department included a 'Chemische Präparaten- und Fabrikaten-Sammlung' (Collection of Chemical Preparations and Manufactured Products), a 'Mathematisches Kabinett' (Mathematical Collection), a 'Physikalisches Kabinett' (Physics Collection), as well as a 'Modellensammlung' (Collection of Models), a 'Mathematische und mechanische Werkstätte' (Mathematical and Mechanical Workshop), a 'Fabriksprodukten-Kabinett' (Collection of Manufactured Products); in its commercial section, it contained a 'Sammlung für Warenkunde' (Collection of Merchandise), the 'Sammlungen der Realschule' (Schools Collections) plus a Collection of Maps.

The Polytechnical Institute's constitution clearly defined the responsibilities of the 'Fabriksprodukten-Kabinett'. In 1816, it had over 6,000 inventory numbers; by 1829, it had over 30,000. In the early 1840s, this originally autonomous collection was merged with Emperor Ferdinand I's collection of products – known as the 'Technisches Kabinett' (Technical Collection) – and other collections to form the 'Technologisches Kabinett' (Technological Collection). In 1912, a total of 19,311 inventory numbers that were no longer required for teaching purposes or 44,341 items were removed from the collection and were loaned to the newly established Technisches Museum.

Foundation and Models

The foundation of the Technisches Museum Wien is closely associated with the work of Wilhelm Franz Exner (1840–1931). Since visiting the Paris Exhibition of 1867, he had been driven by the idea of establishing a large technological museum in Austria. Exner was Professor of Mechanics at the 'Wiener Hochschule für Bodenkultur' and decisively

Max Hegele's award-winning design, Perspective, 1909. Watercolour

influenced the nature of materials testings and standardization in Austria as well as the country's museums and exhibitions.

During the 1873 World Exhibition in Vienna, among the attractions organized by Exner was an 'additional exhibition showing the industry and inventions of Austria'. He hoped to use this varied collection of objects and documents on the history of Austrian industry and inventions as the basis for a technological museum, but was unable to do so. With the support of the 'Niederösterreichischer Gewerbeverein' (Lower Austrian Trade Association), Exner in 1879 founded the 'Technologisches Gewerbemuseum' (Technological Trades Museum). This was the first advanced school of technology in Austria and from the start had a museum attached to it. In line with Exner's ambitions, it focused on timber technology and technological testing. In 1893, again with the support of the Lower Austrian Trade Association, Exner established the 'Museum der Geschichte der österreichischen Arbeit' (Museum of the History of Work in Austria). Richly endowed with items from the Technological Collection, its focus was Austrian technology and industry, and it was affiliated to the 'Technologisches Gewerbemuseum' (Technological Trades Museum).

In parallel with these private institutions, other state-run technological museums were being established, among them, in 1885, the 'k.k. Historisches Museum der österreichischen Eisenbahnen' (Imperial Historical Museum of Austrian Railways); in 1889, the 'k.k. Postmuseum' (Imperial Post Museum); and, in 1890, the 'Gewerbe-hygienisches Museum' (Industrial Hygiene Museum). All of these museums were organizationally distinct entities, were spread across the whole of Vienna and lacked exhibition space. A driving force behind the establishment of the Technisches Museum was the idea that these museums could be housed under one roof.

The Museum can also certainly be regarded as the result of a failed exhibition on industry that was planned to take place in Vienna in 1908 on the occasion of the 60th anniversary of Emperor Franz Joseph I's accession to the throne and which would compete with another exhibition on industry that was already being organized in Prague. The ambitions of the exhibition organizers in Vienna were cleverly re-directed for political reasons. Exner's idea of establishing a permanent Museum of Trade and Industry was again picked up in preference to a temporary exhibition marking the Emperor's jubilee. In June 1907, a 'Vorbereitendes Komitee zur Schaffung eines Technischen Museums für Industrie und Gewerbe in Wien' (Preparatory Committee for the Establishment of a Technological Museum of Trade and Industry in Vienna) was formed that comprised representatives of the city's three industrial federations, the Lower Austrian Trade Association and the Electrotechnical Association. The industrialist Arthur Krupp was elected chairman of the Committee. To secure a financial basis for the project, it was agreed that the state would pay a subsidy of thirty per cent towards the total outlay to a limit of one and a half million crowns. The municipality of Vienna provided the land and made an additional contribution of one million crowns towards the cost of construction. The balance was to be raised through donations.

The Museum under construction, c. 1910. Photograph

A year later, the Committee was replaced by an 'Arbeitsausschuss für die Errichtung des Technischen Museums für Industrie und Gewerbe Wien' (Working Party for the Establishment of a Technological Museum of Trade and Industry in Vienna) which in 1908 issued a document that detailed both progress to date and the main thrust of its programme. Besides the Conservatoire des Arts et Métiers in Paris and London's Science Museum, the main model for the Viennese project was Munich's Deutsches Museum that had been established in 1903. There was an intensive exchange of experiences between Munich and Vienna in the years leading up to the foundation of the Vienna museum, especially between Exner and Oskar von Miller.

The Technisches Museum Wien was to illustrate technological developments in trade and industry and to exhibit their most up-to-date achievements, with preference being given to objects and collections of Austrian provenance. Foreign exhibits were to be displayed only if they played a significant role in the evolution of industrial and commercial production. Moreover, rather than single items, complete series of objects were to be exhibited that illustrated manufacturing or working processes. Besides acquiring objects or reproductions of them, descriptions and publications were also to be collected. To increase the appeal of the museum, talks and specialist exhibitions were planned.

Wilhelm Franz Exner (1840–1931). Oil painting

Ludwig Erhard (1863–1940). Photograph

In 1909, the 'Verein Technisches Museum für Industrie und Gewerbe' (Friends of the Museum of Trade and Industry) was established. It comprised general members, a supervisory body and an executive board supported by a legal advisory body whose 900 members were the representatives of science, industry and commerce as well as the civil service.

Based on a preliminary draft by Emil Ritter von Förster, an architectural competition was held to find a design for the museum building. Twenty-four architects, among them respected practitioners like Max Freiherr von Ferstel, Adolf Loos and Otto Wagner, submitted twenty-seven designs. The winner was Hans Schneider whose design most closely matched that of von Förster who died in 1909. Emperor Franz Joseph I laid the foundation stone in a ceremony on 20 June 1909. For financial reasons, the original design was reduced by two thirds, but construction started in June 1910, and the shell of the building, one of the first reinforced concrete structures in Austria, was completed at the end of 1912, eighteen months behind schedule.

INSTALLATION AND OPENING

Ludwig Erhard (1863–1940) was the first director of the Technisches Museum Wien from 1913 to 1930. He had a decisive influence on the Museum's organization and exhibitions policy and was a keen collector. As early as 1912, the Museum absorbed substantial collections from the public domain, including the 'Gewerbe-hygienisches Museum' (Industrial Hygiene Museum), the 'Technologisches Kabinett' (Technological Collection) of the Technische Hochschule, the 'Museum der Geschichte der österreichischen Arbeit' (Museum of the History of Work in Austria), the 'Salinenverwaltung' (Salt Mines Administration), the 'Sammlung von

Maßen und Gewichten der k.k. Normalausgleichskommission' (Collection of Weight and Measures of the Imperial Committee on Comparison Standards) and the 'Modellensammlung der k.k. Landwirtschaftsgesellschaft' (Collection of Models of the Imperial Agricultural Association). In 1914, the Imperial Railway and Post Office Museums moved into the Museum building, but retained their own administrations until 1980.

A start was made to the installation of exhibits in 1914. The ground floor was given over to Transport; various branches of industry were represented on the first floor and Bridge Construction and Surveying were housed on the second floor. A life-size mock-up of mine workings was created in the basement.

Even before work on the Museum was completely finished, Exner more than anyone insisted that the Museum should open early. With no ceremony, its doors opened to visitors on 6 May 1918. A shortage of staff and funds meant that the remaining exhibition spaces would not be completed for another two decades and would open only gradually.

Guided tour in the Central Hall, after 1918. Photograph

THE MUSEUM AFTER 1918

After 1918, political and economic events crucially influenced developments at the Museum. Having been founded by an Association, the Museum was nationalized in 1922 and was placed under the control of the Federal Ministry of Trade and Industry. In the 1930s, the Museum offered adult education courses and talks about the latest technological innovations.

Second 'Glass model of a brain', made by director Josef Nagler, 1953. Photograph

The 1930s was also the time when the 'Österreichisches Forschungsinstitut für Geschichte der Technik' (Austrian Research Institute for the History of Technology) was given institution status. Formed originally as a private research establishment, the Institute began its work within the Museum on 1 July 1931 under Ludwig Erhard. Freelancers at first supplied it with material on the history of technology. As of 1932, the results of its research and collecting activities were publicised in a journal called *Blätter für Geschichte der Technik* (Journal on the History of Technology), known after 1939 as *Blätter für Technikgeschichte*. The Institute was nationalized and merged with the Museum shortly after Erhard's death in 1940.

After 1938, the body of thought and the terminology associated with National Socialism became increasingly prevalent in the Museum. Immediately after the National Socialists assumed power, discussions were held about the possibility of merging the Museum with the 'Haus der Deutschen Technik' under Fritz Todt. The role envisaged for the Viennese collection was that of carrying 'German Technology' to southeast Europe. Nothing came of the proposed reorganization and construction of an extension to house administrative offices and exhibition space. Following the dissolution of Austrian ministries, the Museum was placed under the direct administrative control of the Reich's governor of Vienna. At the beginning of 1939, Hans Kummerlöwe, the director of Dresden's Zoology Museum, became the scientific director of the Museum of Technology, the Natural History Museum and the Austrian Museum of Folk Life and Folk Art, but held the post for a short time only.

The Museum survived the war years of 1939–45, and the evacuation of its most valuable items, almost undamaged. Once the exhibits had been returned, the Technisches Museum Wien re-opened on 14 October 1945, the first major museum in Vienna to do so.

Unveiling a bust of Nikola Tesla in front of the Museum, 1952. Photograph

Apart from the creation of more exhibition space in the 1950s, only running repairs were carried out on the building well into the 1980s. Come 1992, the building itself was all but a museum piece and the decision was made to carry out a major refurbishment of it.

The Museum re-opened in 1999 and, in line with a law applicable to Federal Museums in Austria, its status on 1 January 2000 became that of a legally autonomous 'Wissenschaftliche Anstalt öffentlichen Rechts des Bundes' (Federal Scientific Institution under public law).
FeM

Erecting the first Kaplan turbine in front of the Museum, 1960. Photograph

The Collection

A place rich in tradition, the Technisches Museum Wien is one of the world's longest-established institutions specializing in dealing with the development of technology and industry. When it was founded, it was able to make use of a number of notable collections inherited from its predecessors. Following the Museum's complete refurbishment and re-opening in 1999, these collections continue to attract visitors. In presenting its collections, the Technisches Museum Wien aims to make technology accessible to a wide variety of visitors through a host of methods with something of appeal to everyone. By setting the unique and historical objects in its collections in their cultural, economic and social contexts, the Museum, in keeping with statutory requirements, aims to give visitors a better understanding of the various fields of technology. It achieves this through modern forms of presentation and by allowing visitors to experience its collections actively in pleasant and welcoming surroundings.

When the Museum was founded, the building itself and the exhibitions within it were intended to give experts and laypeople alike a better understanding of the then latest technology. The function and effects of technical designs and structures were made accessible through working models and experiments. Subjects and exhibits were explained in descriptions and keys. The main focus lay on the development of trade and industry in the 19th century as well as new inventions and installations. Even a century ago, it was important that holdings and exhibitions were as up-to-date as possible. After opening in 1918, it took until the 1930s to finish the installation of the Museum. It was during this phase that the collections that were incomplete or still at the planning stage when the Museum opened, such as the aviation collection, were finally completed. Even in the 1930s, it was obvious that not all the objects that had been transferred to the Museum could be displayed. Certain annexes – among them the administration block and the large banqueting hall – were planned but not built. Their absence was – and continues to be – keenly felt.

Over the following decades, the collections were rearranged as more experience and new insights were gained. In 1968, around 10% of the Museum's holdings were on display to the public. The two independent museums – the Postal Museum and the Railway Museum – that had always been housed within the Technisches Museum Wien were taken over by it in 1980.

A ministerial decision was made to clear the Museum completely at the start of the refurbishment programme. This decision permitted an increase in exhibition space from around 16,000 m² to around 22,000 m² but also gave Museum staff the opportunity to redesign their collections. As it had already done when it was first being fitted out, the Technisches Museum Wien, a long-established science museum with a notable collection of original objects, took account of how comparable institutions – the Conservatoire National des Arts et Métiers in Paris, the Science Museum in London and the Deutsches Museum in Munich – exhibit their holdings and made use of their experiences when planning the re-installation of its own collections. Ideas for the redesign of the Museum's exhibition spaces came not only from these established institutions, however; they were also borrowed from Science Centres where hands-on experiments introduce visitors to the fundamental principles of science. Variously realized, both concepts have now been combined in the permanent collections.

The rethink has not changed the Museum's approach to its original mission but rather enhances it with its ambitious aim of giving visitors a better understanding of the history of technology and society and of the influence technology has on humans and their everyday lives. Visitors are not merely led from one object to another, but instead are encouraged to grasp the connections between the exhibits and to leave with something to think about. One of the declared aims in redesigning the collections was to create a museum of connections. This explains why, at the start of the rethink, the Museum's 30-odd specialist collections were merged to form five, then six, general groups that serve as the basis for exhibition planning even if they do not exactly reflect the structure of the Museum's collections that are now divided as follows:
1. Fundamental Principles of Science and Technology
2. Information and Communications Technology
3. Mining, Mechanical and Electrical Engineering
4. Manual and Industrial Production Engineering
5. Transport
6. Civil Engineering, Everyday Technology and Environmental Technology

The collections allow visitors to set off on a journey of discovery through the history of particular related topics. Such a thorough organizational rethink can be achieved only in several stages, of course. During the first one, 'Nature and Knowledge', 'Images of Technology', 'Heavy Industry' and 'Musical Instruments' opened in summer 1999.

In two parts, 'Nature and Knowledge' is the first exhibition to be visited on Level 1. It contains the section of 'The Fundamental Principles of Science and Technology' that deals with physics. In 'Phenomena and Experiments' in the east wing of the basement, visitors are invited to make sense of physical phenomena for themselves. 'Concepts and Consequences' in the west wing of the basement describes the development of physics.

The central hall on Level 2 houses an exhibition called 'Images of Technology'. It compares the technology of the time the Museum opened with that of today and includes almost all the fields in which the Museum collects. It is followed by an exhibition on 'Heavy Industry' that contains items related to 'Manual and Industrial Production Engineering' as well as the 'Mining, Mechanical and Electrical Engineering'. Mainly comprising items related to the 'Mining, Mechanical and Electrical Engineering', the exhibition on 'Energy' in the eastern side wing opened in autumn 1999.

The central section of Level 3 contains a multipurpose space for exhibitions and events. In the exhibition 'Mass-Produced Luxury Goods' on the western side wing gallery valuable pieces from the 'Manual and Industrial Production Engineering' collection are displayed. Focusing on the relationship between humans and technology, a permanent exhibition entitled 'Everyday Life – Directions for Use' has been open in the eastern side wing since autumn 2005. Most of its exhibits are from the 'Civil Engineering, Everyday Technology and Environmental Technology' collection. Also in the eastern side wing, a 'Mini' Museum has been open for youngsters since 2000.

In the central section of Level 4, the exhibition on 'Musical Instruments' illustrates the interplay between music and science.

An exhibition called 'medien.welten' opened in the western side wing in spring 2003. Containing items from the collection of 'Information and Communications Technology', which now includes the holdings of the former Postal Museum, it examines the history of the storage and transmission of information. On the subject of 'Transport', the eastern side wing contains a number of highlights: large, original motor vehicles and aircraft, as well as old and valuable models of them. With the support of the 1. Österreichischer Straßen- und Eisenbahn Klub, however, the Railway Museum at Strasshof in Lower Austria exhibits and operates parts of this collection.

LaH, TrM

View from the entrance hall up to the facade of the museum.

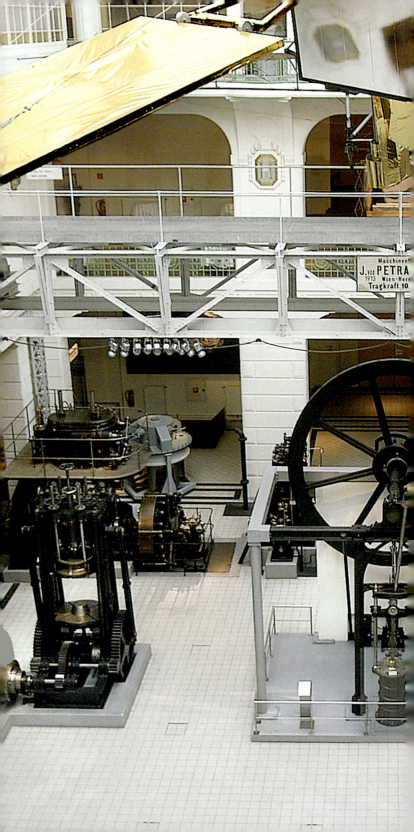

Images of Technology

Images of Technology

When it opened in 1918, the Technisches Museum Wien showcased the most advanced technology of the day. First and foremost, it covered the age of industrialization in the 19th century. This in itself produced a specific image of technology: engines, large power generation units, heavy machine tools and new means of transport such as railways and the first aircraft were all symbols of an era that wholeheartedly embraced innovation. The excitement that technology produced at the time found expression in the representative objects displayed in the museum's Central Hall which itself was a reflection of the latest technology. The aim was to create an atmospheric space in which to display the best technical achievements of the day.

Having reopened in 1999 after a complete refurbishment, the museum now reflects 20th century developments in technology and the way its look has changed. The museum's Central Hall now illustrates the transition from an industrial to an information society, with the Images of Technology that predominated in 1918 and 1999 placed side by side. On display at the rear of the hall, examples of large machines from the transport and industry collections represent the image of technology that prevailed when the museum was founded. They are contrasted in the front part of the hall with the image of technology that prevails now, one that is essentially influenced by the virtual world and immateriality of digital media. Data processing and media networks are becoming increasingly crucial in the manufacture and transport of goods. The transport networks of the past are the media networks of today, and with industrial mass production comes mass data processing.

The Steam Engine

The steam engine is regarded as the chief element of the Industrial Revolution. It exceeded human output of work many times over and, unlike windmills or watermills, could be used everywhere and at any time given an adequate supply of fuel. Early steam engines were particularly used to pump water out of mines, but they soon found widespread use as a source of power elsewhere. The steam engine on display in the museum's Central Hall, for instance, was in use from 1856 in the Dreher'sche Brewery in Klein-Schwechat near Vienna. Via a belt pulley, it drove the brewery's main transmission shaft from which V-belts in turn drove numerous machines. The steam engine and the use of new machine tools increased the speed of production processes and led to their concentration in factories. Standardization, Taylorization and the introduction of the assembly line in the 20th century were essential prerequisites for mass production and mass consumption.

The Steam Locomotive

The transport of goods long depended on beasts of burden with their limited carrying capacity. The advent of the steam engine opened up new possibilities in goods transport, however. From 1832, the 'k.k. privilegierte erste Eisenbahn-Gesellschaft' operated a horse-drawn railway between Linz and Budweis. From 1836, the route was operated from Gmunden via Linz to Budweis. In 1855, ten steam-powered trains began operating between Linz and Gmunden, among them the 'Gmunden' on display here. Belching out acrid smoke, 'iron horses' elsewhere subsequently began to haul heavier loads than had ever before been possible. In addition, they carried more and more passengers, divided into three classes: aristocratic or wealthy bourgeois holidaymakers, commercial travellers and workers. The royal trains were surely the epitome of luxury travel. Built in Prague in 1873, the royal saloon car allowed

Steam engine from the Dreher'sche Brewery. Inv. No. 688

The 'Gmunden' steam engine and coach B10 of the 'k.k. privilegierte erste Eisenbahn-Gesellschaft' (First Imperial and Royal Railway Company). Inv. Nos. 40.395, 40.520

Empress Elisabeth to travel in peace and comfort. A dense network of railways was gradually developed that connected centres of heavy industry and rapidly growing cities.

What steam locomotives did on land, steamships did at sea. They carried not only raw materials and goods but also wealthy passengers and emigrants.

The imperial saloon car built for the Empress Elisabeth, HZ 0011. Inv. No. 40.331

Flying Machines

Transport networks on land and sea were soon followed by transport networks in the air. Suspended from the glazed roof is an Etrich II 'Taube' (Dove), a motorized glider that was built in the winter of 1909/10 by Igo Etrich in Wiener Neustadt. Winged seeds were the inspiration for the aircraft's wings. On 17 May 1910, this flying machine made the first long-distance, cross-country flight from Wiener Neustadt to Vienna and back. It went into serial production at Lohner in Vienna and the Imperial and Royal Air Corps (Luftfahrttruppe) in Fischamend. Although they were initially intended only for military purposes such as reconnaissance over enemy territory, such flying machines soon found commercial applications. Compared with trains and ships, they had only a limited carrying capacity, but they were much faster over long distances. They soon became important for the scheduled transport of mail and passengers.

The Etrich II 'Taube' (Dove), 1910. Inv. No. 1.933

Communications Satellite

The global reach of communications in today's westernized information societies is based on a worldwide network comprising various elements: cable networks are used mainly in conurbations; radio networks cover medium to long distances; and satellites serve as relay stations for communications between the northern and southern hemispheres. Suspended from the glazed roof is a model of an Artemis research satellite ('Advanced Relay and Technology Mission Satellite') of the European Space Agency. An Ariane 5 launcher put the original into orbit around

Images of Technology 23

Model of the 'Artemis' communications satellite. Inv. No. 50.090

the earth in 2001 to test new developments in telecommunications, including a network of fixed ground stations, mobile land vehicles and European railways. Besides conventional radio transmissions, a more efficient form of data transmission between satellites that uses light in the form of lasers is being tested. Extraterrestrial data transmission has many uses: telephony, radio and television broadcasts, navigation, earth observation and, of course, espionage and other military applications.

Television control desk

Television is one of the most important elements in the system of electronic media that developed in the 20th century. By means of a global telecommunications network, images of events are reproduced on viewers' screens around the world. Besides entertainment, sport and culture, there is television coverage of events that are significant in politics and economics. Television programmes are produced in studios to where events filmed by outside cameras are beamed and mixed with archive and live studio footage. The presenter and the streaming pictures are 'merged' in what is known as a Blue Box. The control desk exhibited here belonged to Austrian Radio and was used from 1985 in television production at the ORF-Zentrum on Vienna's Küniglberg. The camera filmed studio images, the character generator produced inserts and various sources delivered other input. The various elements were mixed at the control desk to form the complete television image that was then broadcast to viewers.

Invisible Person

Computers symbolize today's information society in which electronics and digital technology are now the tools that allow the mass processing of data in the form of numbers, script, sound or images. In the reproduction of life-like moving images, especially three-dimensional ones, a vast amount of data processing is required. Each image consists of millions of pixels, and each sequence of a moving image consists of numerous single images. Within fractions of seconds, computers capture vast amounts of data, process them according to predetermined criteria and reproduce them. The interactive installation known as the 'Invisible Person' enables visitors to interact directly with a computer-generated figure. Visitors' gestures and movements are recorded on camera and transmitted to a computer. The computer-generated figure reacts to visitors' external stimuli through actions of its own and expresses emotional states by changing the shape and colour of its surface.
MoO, PeW

1980s control desk from ORF Austrian Television. Inv. No. 50.587

Nature and Knowledge

Nature and Knowledge
From Phenomena to Concepts

A view of 'Phenomena and Experiments'

THE CONCEPT IN BRIEF

Technology is now unthinkable without the fundamental principles of science. This was not always the case, however. Empirical solutions with no verifiable theoretical basis were also at the forefront of medicine, for instance. The systematic application of the natural sciences, whose methods were developed from the 17th century onwards, reduced time-consuming scientific developments by means of trial and error.

How can knowledge be gained from nature? Philosophy and mythology represent the oldest human attempts to interpret phenomena. Consistently verifiable results that led to permanent changes in human thinking and behaviour were not achieved until the era of the methods developed by the natural sciences, however. Nowadays these methods are of global significance and are applied comprehensively in the fields of pure research, trade and industry, medicine and, unfortunately, weapons technology. This is the reason why natural sciences have a special responsibility to bear. Physics as a leading science is the main focus of this exhibition.

The department is divided into two sections. 'Phenomena and Experiments' is aimed at visitors keen to experience things for themselves, while 'Concepts and Consequences' is for those who want to learn how scientific knowledge is developed and where it is applied.

Phenomena and Experiments

Experimentation is one of science's most important methods of investigating unknown phenomena. Using a number of experiments, visitors can try for themselves to get to the bottom of things in this exhibition with its seven main topics inviting them to explore questions that are of importance in the Museum's other departments. Visitors choose for themselves the order in which they go round the exhibition; what counts here is curiosity about phenomena and how they are explained.

Can our senses judge objectively?

Why do we need measuring instruments? Our brain calculates distances and speeds, weights and sizes at lightning speed, and without our conscious intervention. It compares the information it must interpret with what it already knows from experience and assesses its significance. This 'survival programme' functions in our usual surroundings, but fails us in situations that do not correspond to patterns we have already learned. This results in misjudgements that cannot be used for scientific evidence. Accurate measuring equipment is therefore needed if results are to be verifiable. Experiments show how our perception can be deceived.

In the 'Distortion Room', visitors will see just how relative estimates of size can be. The 'Cheshire cat' demonstrates the function of attention in the brain.

A shared discovery: fascination for young and old alike

Enter the Blue Box and find yourself in a TV weather studio, an aquarium or other projected environments. Inv. No. 29.000

What is real, what is imaginary?

The boundary between reality (as it can be experienced objectively) and (artificially created) fiction can be moved using technical means. A harmless instance would be a diversionary tactic, a conjuring trick, say, intended to entertain. It could also be an illusion that one is unaware of, created for instance using image editing or the 'Blue Box'. What is reality? What is fiction? You would be well advised not to take the images you see at face value.

Our experiments demonstrate a number of easily understandable technological methods to create illusions. Visitors can see themselves in front of a number of backgrounds in the 'Blue Box', or they may create short animations by themselves or watch professional ones at a media station.

Images – Documents and Perspectives

As a source of information, images are usually more direct than words. Pre-historic and ancient cave paintings clearly illustrate the point. Pictures help us understand contexts, for instance in instructions. Certainly since the invention of photography, pictures have often been the only records that exist of events. If interpreted correctly, they are objective, but certain constraints do change the information content of pictures. For example, the size of objects in photographs cannot be judged accurately without knowing the distance between the photographer and his subject and the focal length. Computer technology allows changes to be made to pictures – to the extent, indeed, that they can be falsified. Impressions of depth and solidity are achieved using stereoscopy, and colour impressions can largely be changed.

Changing Colours of Images: What happens to the overall impression? Inv. No. 50.598

Force – an Important Aspect of Technology and our Everyday Lives

Force is omnipresent and is involved in almost every action. An armchair, for instance, reacts with force when we sit down on it; if it did not do so, we would collapse on the ground. However, in our everyday lives, we pay no attention to most of these mechanisms.

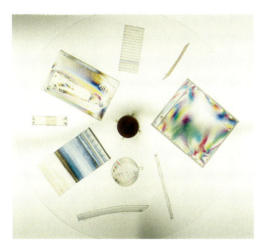

Photoelasticity reveals different strains in different colours. Inv. No. 50.339

Force manifests itself only in its effects: bodies are distorted or change their momentum when force is exerted. Pressure is also a force, one that acts on the unit area of a surface. Force exists both in the subatomic context and the astronomical dimensions between heavenly bodies and distant galaxies. It is fair to say that force literally holds the world together.

Our air cushion table illustrates the effects of diminished frictional force; here, polarized light reveals the areas of stress in transparent bodies.

Nature and Knowledge

Vibrations and Waves

There are no rigid bodies or stationary states in nature. Where elasticity and variable forces are at work, vibrations can develop. If they spread, we call them waves. Some examples of waves are simple mechanical vibrations, caused by jolts, say, or sound waves, alternating currents or even light. Their shared characteristics include, for instance, reflection or superimposition. Using vibrations, substances or processes can be analysed, news can be transmitted, distances can be measured (e.g. echo sounding) and they can be used for ultrasonic cleaning. They are sometimes so rich in energy that they can destroy objects. In our exhibition, a large 'wave machine' gives a slow-motion demonstration of wave propagation, while sound propagation in tubes is demonstrated by a Kundt's tube.

The 'Wave Machine' demonstrates how vibrations spread in a medium. Inv. No. 50.342

Electromagnetism

There is a causal relation between electricity and magnetism. Each can be changed into the other, a fact known to us for some 200 years. They have since been regarded as one phenomenon that we call 'electromagnetism'. Our knowledge of it has opened the way to diverse applications in electrotechnology. We cannot now imagine life without generators, electric motors, transformers, relays, eddy-current brakes or lifting magnets, for instance. The forces acting between currents and magnets, such as those in cathode ray tubes, also belong to this group of phenomena. Even the ignition spark in petrol engines is generated electromagnetically.

An experiment using a transformer demonstrates the convertibility of alternating currents and the magnetic field of currents is demonstrated by means of powdered iron.

The 'Transformer Experiment' explains the relationship between electric current, voltage and power. Inv. No. 50.726

Currents and Electrons

Electrons are among the elementary particles that constitute atoms. Electric current in cables consists of these particles. With nerve, brain and heart function also relying on electrical activity, an exact understanding of conduction is essential in the field of medicine, too.

A great deal of energy conduction occurs today through cables and electrical wiring. The energy levels range from the glow of a lamp to the striking of lightning. Electrons also play a major role in communication and data processing. Examples of conduction in the human body are provided by an electrocardiogram and the measurement of the electric tension between metal plates and the palms.

The 'Electrocardiogram Experiment' demonstrates the electric nature of muscle movement. Inv. No. 50.759

Nature and Knowledge 33

Concepts and Consequences

How are natural processes explained? Science asks fundamental questions about them and, by applying specific methods, develops universally valid concepts that shape our understanding of nature and often lead to new procedures and ways of thinking. Science thus has far-reaching consequences for every aspect of our lives.

Presented in the long corridor immediately behind the entrance, the central theme of this exhibition is the development of cosmology, the science of the origin and development of the universe. In adjacent rooms, visitors will find displays on important principles or fundamental discoveries that correspond to the stages of cosmological development. Cosmology has always been influenced by scientific progress, especially

A view of 'Concepts and Consequences'

in physics, and vice versa. Both strands converge in 'The Century of Physics', the 20th.

The First Exact Science: Astronomy

Astronomy is the study of heavenly bodies. Man first made astronomical observations more than 6,000 years ago. For long periods in human history, astronomy was closely associated with mythological ideas about man's place in the universe. Practical issues also played a role, however: how were humans to divide the calender, calculate the time of day or find their bearings? As the first 'exact science', astronomy greatly influ-

Towards a heliocentric view: The system of experiment and theory was developed at the same time. The exhibition tells this in two story lines

enced the development of physics, and its status increased in the second half of the 20th century thanks to space technology and new theories about the origins of the universe.

From Observations to Conceptions of the World
The beginnings of astronomy are found in the observations of the stars made in ancient Egypt and Mesopotamia dating back to third millennium BC. They were further processed in ancient Greece using geometric models and summarized by Ptolemy in the second century AD. According to his findings, the Sun and planets revolved around the static Earth. Arab astronomers in the Middle Ages again spread knowledge of the 'Ptolemaic system' throughout Europe. As it explained every observation and was consistent with Roman Catholic doctrine, it was widely accepted.

Nicolaus Copernicus (1473–1543), on the other hand, maintained that the Earth and the planets revolved around the static Sun. Initially, his work aroused little interest and was merely seen as a mathematical aid for making improvements to the calender. Galileo Galilei (1564–1642) later championed Copernicus' theory, which in the course of the 17th century gained acceptance as a realistic description of the solar system. Using new observations, Johannes Kepler (1571–1630) further developed the theory.

Philipp Imsser's magnificent astronomical clock is the key object in this part of the exhibition. Constructed from 1554–59 to demonstrate the movements of the heavenly bodies, it is geocentric, i.e. the planets, Sun and Moon revolve around the static Earth. It was used to establish the positions of the stars at any time and to calculate the occurrence of eclipses and certain phenomena of the Moon. It could even be used in astrological interpretations! In contrast, an orrery by Henry Pyefinch, *c.* 1780, demonstrates the heliocentric model.

Astronomy Becomes a Power Factor

In the past, astronomy was closely associated with religious and mythological ideas. The controversy surrounding Copernicus' theory is clear proof of that. Yet there was always also a practical side to it: observations of the Sun were used to divide time into years, the years into seasons, the days into hours. Mechanical clocks in the 17th century still had to be regularly set by sundials as they were so inaccurate. Astronomical observations were important in navigation as a means of fixing a ship's position and also complemented compass bearings. This was significant for the development of astronomy because navigation became a crucial power factor in the conflicts between European states over colonies and trade routes. To improve astronomy further, nations built observatories in the 17th century so as to obtain more accurate surveys of the Earth and the night sky. The newly acquired knowledge led to the manufacture of ever more accurate globes such as Cary's terrestrial and celestial globe from the early 19th century.

The Foucault pendulum in the Museum restaurant marks a milestone in man's knowledge of the Earth. Jean Bernard Léon Foucault conducted a fundamental experiment in the Paris Panthéon on 8 January 1851. By allowing a long pendulum to swing freely, he showed that the rotation of the plane of the pendulum's swing can only be explained by the Earth's rotation.

The belief that the Earth was a solid sphere had to be abandoned when continental drift was discovered. The geological changes in the Earth's surface over millions of years can be retraced on a computer screen.

Physics Changes Astronomy

How did the planetary system evolve? How does the Sun produce heat? Which chemical elements are present in stars? Physical questions such as these changed astronomy in the 19th century. 'Astrophysics' was born, a science whose research methods were adapted to such new questions. Especially in observatories built at the end of the 19th century, instruments and techniques of physics made their entry. At the beginning of the 20th century, the theories underlying astronomy were changed fundamentally when Albert Einstein (1879–1955) published his General Theory of Relativity. It put the question of the origins and development of the universe on an entirely new basis. Of the various theories that were subsequently developed in an attempt to answer Einstein's

A changing world-view: Kepler's first thoughts on the design of the universe in model form are opposed to demonstration equipment based on the heliocentric model

question, the one known as the Big Bang Theory became generally accepted.

The space age began after 1945 using the rocket technology developed by the military in World War II. In a wholly new way, astronomy now had practical applications, both military and civilian.

Greatly improved telescopes were one of the prerequisites for the development of astrophysics. On display is a 10-foot reflecting telescope by Friedrich Wilhelm Herschel, *c.* 1790.

Using a spark chamber built by Vienna's Institute for High-Energy Physics in 1999, visitors can view the cosmic radiation that Victor Franz Hess discovered in 1911. The fragment of moon rock on display is a 'memento' of a more recent moon landing.

How is scientific knowledge developed?

Scientific knowledge is the product of the interplay between experiment and theory. In experiments, natural processes are not only observed, but are also investigated and modified in the laboratory under controlled conditions. In this way, new phenomena can be produced that would not otherwise occur in nature. A mathematical analysis of the results of experiments is performed and compared with the theory that

Nature and Knowledge   37

The development of the theory of light

can be expanded or modified as required. Theory allows scientists to predict new phenomena that in turn are investigated in experiments.

Atwood's Machine was used to demonstrate the falling process in slow motion.

Newton's 'Crucial Experiment' proves that spectral colours have no further components. Visitors can test it for themselves. A prism spectroscope by Adam Hilger, formerly owned by Auer von Welsbach, works with colour break-up of light for material analysis.

What is the effect of physical forces?
Force is a key concept in physics, and ideas about how it works have changed throughout history. In the 19th century, the term 'field' came to be used to describe electromagnetic forces. A field is a defined region in which certain measurement is assigned to each point. In field theory, physicists consider the influence of the field on individual particles rather than the interaction in the field between particles. All the fundamental theories in physics nowadays are 'field theories'. Scientists have yet to achieve a 'grand unified theory' (GUT) encompassing every type of force.

Three experiments devised by Michael Faraday demonstrate the effects of electromagnetic fields and are fundamental to the subsequent development of electromagnetic theory.

What is matter?

Matter is composed of tiny, indivisible particles known as atoms. At the beginning of the 19th century, this idea was used as an explanation for chemical reactions. This prompted an intensive study of atomic theory which became ever more important in physics, too. Following the discovery of the electron in 1897, scientists conjectured that still smaller particles existed within the atom whose exact structure was identified almost 40 years later: protons and neutrons form the nucleus, electrons the shell. The search for the basic building blocks of matter was not yet finished, however, and continues to this day.

The mass spectrometer on display was used, among other things, to analyse isotopic mixtures; the late 19th-century analytical balance was used to determine the mass of samples.

How can physical processes be analysed?

What is the state at the beginning of a process and what is the state on its completion? In an analysis of physical processes, these are the two

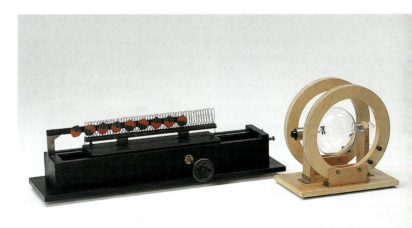

Invisible forces: The demonstration and application of magnetic force using selected examples

questions usually asked. What were the 'fundamental constants' – in other words, what properties remained constant? Throughout history, scientists have sought conservation laws of universal application. Some examples are the conservation of mass in chemical reactions, the conservation of momentum in elastic collision processes and the conservation of energy. Conservation laws are still very important in physics

Spout and deflection unit of the mass spectrometer MM6o. Inv. No. 66.166

today. If possible, they are deduced from superordinated symmetry principles.

Despite our knowledge of the law of conservation of energy, attempts are still made to create a perpetual motion machine. The perpetuum mobile exhibited in the Museum is a copy of the original in the Prague Museum of Technology.

The 1916 apparatus for the determination of the mechanical equivalent of heat after Puluj, a former professor at Prague's Institute of Science, was used to determine the conversion factor between mechanical and heat energy.

Why is the theory of heat so important?

Heat is a form of energy. Both this fundamental law of physics and the fundamentals of the theory of heat were formulated around 1850. It developed from weather observations and attempts to gain a better understanding of the workings of the steam engine.

Another fundamental law is that heat is always only transferred from a body or system that is hot to one that is cold. In other words, certain physical processes occur only in one direction in time ('irreversibility').

No similar restriction exists in any other physical theory. On account of this peculiarity and its wide validity, the theory of heat is an extremely important branch of physics.

The heat pump utilizes the theory of heat to transfer heat mechanically: its temperature is increased or decreased depending on the way its crank is turned.

Johann Natterer's apparatus for the liquefaction of carbon dioxide, constructed by Joseph Schembor *c.* 1817, harnesses the property of gases, under sufficient pressure, to liquefy below their critical temperature. The application of the theory of thermodynamics allows engineers to construct refrigerating plants capable of extreme temperatures as low as -190°C, the temperature required for the liquefaction of air.

A model demonstrating the conversion of energy. From the Museum's installation in 1918, it is proof for the didactic demand to explain important scientific principles to the general public. Inv. No. 10.598

Why did scientific education become so important?

Railways, telegraphy and electrification profoundly changed people's lives in the 19th century. Science was seen as the foundation of these technological inventions and grew steadily in importance. To promote acceptance of the new technologies, science had to explain to society the principles underlying them and to present a rational picture of the

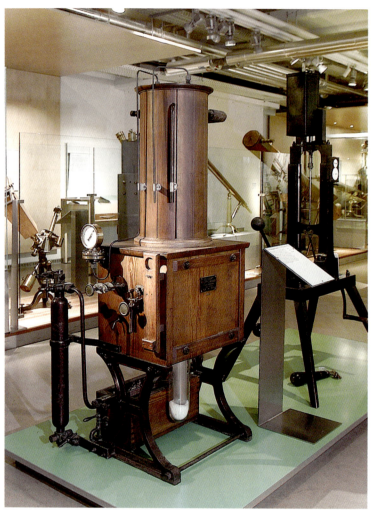

An air liquefaction apparatus by Linde, 1901. The application of theoretical thermodynamics made the construction of refrigerators down to −190 °C – the temperature to liquefy air – possible. Inv. No. 13.773

world. To do this, more scientists and engineers were needed. Schools and newly established institutions such as the Technisches Museum Wien thus strengthened their commitment to disseminating scientific knowledge at the turn of the last century.

Exhibits from the Museum's original installation illustrate the teaching methods used in technological education in the early 20th century.

What is radiation?

Radiation is energy that travels in the form of electromagnetic waves or particles. Light, heat radiation and radio waves were known examples at the end of the 19th century. The term now used every day owes more to

X-rays and radioactivity that were discovered in 1895 and 1896 respectively. The surprising properties of the newly discovered rays caused a sensation. Besides having many practical applications, especially in medicine, the rays were also used by physicists in experiments, for instance in analyses of crystals. At the same time, however, it was also recognised that radiation was dangerous to humans.

An X-ray apparatus from around 1925 and a whole-body X-ray plate from the University of Vienna's Anatomy Department from 1913 represent the rapid development of the medical application of X-rays after their discovery. Museum visitors can experiment with radioactive samples taken from the environment.

How exactly can physical phenomena be calculated?

All physical phenomena can be predicted exactly because complex natural processes can be reduced to basic phenomena. We now know that this supposition is not always valid, however. For instance, if all the reci-

Equipment that led to the discovery of X-rays

procal forces of attraction are taken into account, the planetary orbits cannot be calculated exactly. In the theory of heat, precise assertions may be made only about a large number of atoms, but not about individual atoms. The findings of quantum theory further restrict the possibilities of prediction. Yet even such 'coincidental' or 'chaotic' phenomena can be described according to the laws of nature.

The display on 'Calculable Nature' is intended to show the changes of this view. Astronomy – symbolized here by the telescope – was held to be the model for the other sciences. The precision achieved by astronomy in prediction was to be applied to investigations of all natural processes – from observations of the tiniest particles in a 'dust counter' to the visualized movements of atomic particles in cloud chambers.

The cause of random Brownian Motion is demonstrated using an air cushion table. An artist's interpretation of this is Bernard Gitton's 'Chaotic Fountain' at the stairs leading into the Central Hall.

The century of physics

The 20th century was the century of physics. Quantum theory and the theory of relativity contradicted established science at the beginning of the century and changed our ideas about space, time and causality. The new conception of the world occasioned by physics fascinates many laypeople even today. Physics became more mathematical and more abstract, and the interconnections between physics and the military and industry became ever closer.

The atom bomb provided a vivid example of the enormous power of physics. In research laboratories, (usually large) teams of scientists developed the new technologies without which modern industrial society would be unthinkable.

20th-century theories are applied in semiconductors, lasers and high-energy physics. Semiconductors are manufactured using monocrystal silicon. The helium-neon-laser on display was one of the first large units of its kind in Austria, and the head of a Betatron particle accelerator was used until quite recently in the Vienna General Hospital.

The end of physics?

At the end of the 19th century, many scientists believed that the chapter on physics was closed except for the odd question of detail. As developments showed, they were wrong. Quantum theory and the theory of relativity fundamentally changed the science. Moreover, in chaos theory, the 20th century gave rise to a completely new field of research. We, too, should expect new developments, together with additions and modifications to existing theories, experimental possibilities and applications. Visitors to the Technisches Museum Wien are therefore also presented with the latest research findings.

DoP

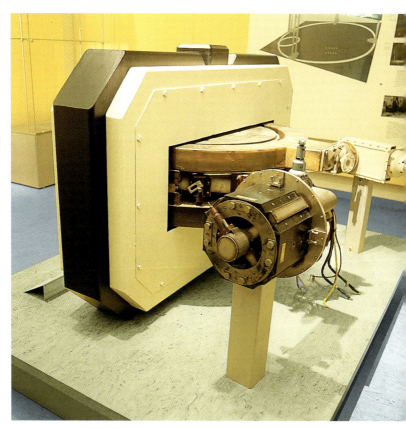

The application of high-energy physics: a particle accelerator (Betatron) from the Vienna General Hospital. Its high-energy electrons were used in post-operative cancer treatment. Inv. No. 28.339

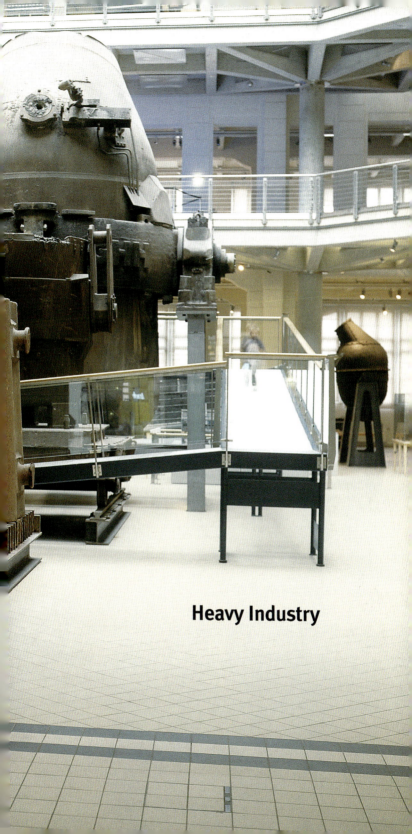

Heavy Industry

Heavy Industry

Basic oxygen process crucible, Oberhausen, 1952. One of the first two crucibles made by the Gutehoffnung steel plant in Oberhausen (Ruhr) and put into operation by VOEST in Linz at the end of 1952. Inv. No. 50.392

The basics

The 'Heavy Industry' exhibition in the west wing of the ground floor examines 'Mining' together with 'Metal Production' and 'Metal Processing'. Large machines are the main exhibits here; they are followed by the theme named 'Leading Sector Steel', a consideration of the economic and social importance of heavy industry in the 20th century.

The exhibition explores the importance of mining and the iron and steel industry in Austria both in the past and present, particularly in the province of Upper Styria where in 1881 the long-established 'Innerberger Hauptgewerkschaft' was incorporated as the Österreichisch-Alpine

Montangesellschaft (ÖAMG, Austrian-Alpine Coal and Iron Mining Company), with its main plant at Donawitz. Following the forced merger with the 'Hermann Göring' Works in Linz, founded in 1938, the group of companies has traded under the name of VOEST-ALPINE AG since 1973. After 1948, Austria's iron and steel works were central to the country's nationalized industry that had largely been rebuilt with financial aid from the Marshall Plan. The industry had a lasting influence on the Austrian economy.

Having been a leading sector of industrialization for over a century, the iron and steel industry in the so-called 'first world' quickly became obsolete. Following closures, redundancies, privatisation and a shift towards higher-value finishing processes, the industry has changed and reduced capacity worldwide, but has, in the former industrialized countries, secured new markets for itself with innovative products.

On a secondary level, the exhibition is arranged mainly according to technical criteria in keeping with the Museum's history and its place internationally. It considers 19 main topics that are familiar to visitors from the Museum's technological specializations and collections. On yet another level, the exhibition looks at 90-odd themes. Topics and different dimensions of technology are thus placed in some kind of order. It is here that political, economic, social and cultural aspects are considered.

Mining

Since humans first established settlements during the New Stone Age, mining has provided them with the resources that became the material basis of the environments they created for themselves and which since industrialization have also supplied their energy needs. Mining is thus an essential prerequisite of civilization. Not only metal-bearing ores are mined, but also salt, coal, minerals for use in industry such as china clay, talc, graphite or magnesite; limestone, gravel and sand, for instance, are quarried for use in construction.

The conditions surrounding the extraction of mineral substances are considered in the first part of the exhibition. Nature has distributed raw materials unevenly across the Earth's surface, and this explains the concentration of mining in particular areas. Only few mineral deposits can be mined profitably.

An interactive computer station created by the Geological Survey of Austria and the Supreme Mining Authority informs visitors about more than 3,000 raw material deposits in Austria. The size and quality of the deposits determine the length of time they can be worked. Mineral deposits are not renewable and are eventually exhausted. The extraction of raw materials brings man to direct confrontation with nature, with resultant dangers both for man and the environment. This is especially true of the advance into even greater depths in underground mining. Mining conditions have given rise over the centuries to a unique mining culture as well as to the early scientific treatment and professional organization of mining techniques, administration and law. The home of the science and culture of mining in Austria is Montan Universität Leoben in Styria that was founded in 1840.

Until the 19th century, the production of metals from ores was a leading sector of the coal and steel industry. Across the world, mining activity has been changed since the mid-19th century first by a shift to coal min-

Selection of miners' lamps from two millennia

ing and then, since the mid-20th century, by a shift towards the extraction of hydrocarbons, as well as the production of raw materials for construction – a special feature of industrialized countries that were once characterized by ore mining.

Starting in early modern times, European mining boomed for over four centuries. In particular, the underground mining of ore and coal, but also opencast mining, came up against limiting geological, economic and ecological factors. If the second half of the 20th century was characterized by a move away from an industrial society to a service economy, in industrialized countries, this was paralleled by the loss of the esteem that society had originally accorded the extraction of raw materials as a vehicle of progress.

After the centuries-old exploitation of deep, productive deposits in industrialized countries, mining across the world since the 19th century has shifted to developing countries. Moreover, the inhabitants of the

The first electric locomotive for use in pits during the Habsburg monarchy, Ganz & Co., Budapest, 1891. It was used in the tunnels of the lead and zinc mine at Bleiberg (Carinthia).
Inv. No. 7.562

consuming countries have, since the onset of industrialization, very much lived at the expense of local populations and the environment in producing countries, which are largely situated in the economically disadvantaged southern hemisphere. During this period of change, an accident happened in 1998 in the Styrian talc mine at Lassing. The disaster cost ten lives and signalled the start of a wide public debate about the function of mining within Austrian society.

Mining must fulfil three basic requirements: firstly, mineral deposits have to be located in the Earth's crust and investigated (prospecting and exploration); secondly, they have to be excavated; and finally, the material obtained must be processed into a product that will find a ready market. At the heart of the 'art of mining' is the removal of mineral substances from the ground, achieved either in shafts underground or in opencast mines. The former method may be long-established, but in recent decades, the latter method has increasingly found favour across large parts of Europe. This is reflected among other things by the huge increase in mining activity in quarries and gravel pits. Austria consumes about 100 million metric tons of raw materials annually – about 13 metric tons per head of population. An average mining depth of 10–15 metres means an annual requirement of 500 hectares of land – the equivalent of 700 football fields!

In what is today Austria, there have always been a number of famous ore, salt and coal mines. One of them is Mitterberg am Hochkönig in the province of Salzburg, a mine worked for copper even 4,000 years ago and that was in operation, with interruptions, until it closed in 1977. Schwaz in Tyrol was one of the world's pre-eminent copper and silver mining areas in the 16th century. In Bleiberg in Carinthia, lead and zinc were mined until 1993; at Hüttenberg in Carinthia, iron ore was mined until 1978. The most famous mine, one that is still in operation, is situated on Erzberg in Styria; the Museum has a large historical model of it on display. Ever since the Middle Ages, the significance of the Alpine

Model of the Erzberg, Cologne, c. 1913. Presented to the Museum on its opening by the 'Österreichisch-Alpine Montangesellschaft' (Austrian Alpine Coal and Iron Mining Company), it shows just how important the industry was to Styria. Inv. No. 9.706/1–2

mining industry is found on the Erzberg, with the state-run Innerberger Hauptgewerkschaft.

Since the early 1990s, brown coal (lignite) has been mined in opencast operations only at Bärnbach in Styria for use in power generation.

As with ore mining, there is a long tradition of salt mining in the Alps, although it is different in several respects. Salt-bearing minerals in the ground were usually extracted using water. The brine was then brought to the surface and pumped to boiling rooms where it was evaporated in large saltpans. The salt deposits were removed from the pans, dried and loaded onto carts ready to be taken away.

In the 20th century, energy-saving thermo-compression techniques superseded saltpans, while borehole brine extraction replaced conventional leaching chambers. Besides being essential for the regulation of the human metabolism, salt also has applications in industry, especially in the manufacture of plastics.

Especially in metal ore mining, a crucial stage exists between extraction of the deposit and the production of crude metal: ore dressing or mineral processing. At this stage, the mined material is crushed, valueless material (gangue) is removed and the ore is enriched. Crushing is performed in stamp mills, mills or crushing plants.

The most important separation processes utilize the physical properties of materials, for instance their specific weight or magnetism. Gangue, waste material containing no ore, is separated and stored. Processing increases the ore content and the material is conveyed to the smelting plant.

Major mines such as the Erzberg, but also smaller pits and smelting plants, all usually in remote locations, required complex logistics to ensure a steady supply of wood as pit timber and as fuel for horizontal and circular charcoal kilns. An additional problem is that access to large

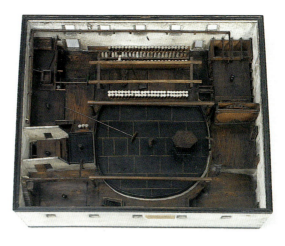

Model of a saltpan, Hall in Tyrol, 17th century. Riveted together from metal plates, these containers held brine that was heated and evaporated to gain salt.
Inv. No. 9.563

wooded areas in the Alps is difficult. Logs were often rafted or driven downriver, but because rivers and streams frequently lacked sufficient water, they were dammed. When the barrage was opened, the surge of water carried the logs with it.

Starting in the mid-19th century, coal superseded wood and charcoal as the energy source in ore smelting, although peat was used for decades at the time, especially in Styrian and Carinthian puddling furnaces.

Women manually sorting ore from valueless material (gangue) at the Erzberg, Styria, c. 1930

Metal Manufacture

Iron is by far the most important metal. It does not occur in nature in pure form, but combined with ores (iron oxides). Iron is reduced in blast furnaces, i.e. it is released from chemical combination with oxygen. As pig iron contains up to 4 per cent carbon, it is brittle and thus has limited uses as a material. It is normally used to make cast iron. If the carbon content is below 2 per cent, the product is known as steel, which can be forged, rolled or drawn.

Iron

The oldest method of iron production is the bowl furnace process hearth, originally clay-lined holes in the ground. By building over them, shaft furnaces up to 2 metres in height were created. The air required for combustion was introduced through clay nozzles, at first using natural draft (fall winds) and later using bellows. Charcoal was used as the fuel and reducing agent.

An original-size bowl furnace process hearth modelled on an archaeological find from a field on Erzberg conveys some idea of how wrought

Cross section of a free-standing coke-fired blast furnace, Witkowitz/Vitkovice, c. 1900. From the 1870s on, such furnaces gradually replaced older charcoal-fired furnaces. Inv. No. 9.781

Furnace air blower, Mariazell, 1847. This cylindrical blower with balancier was in use in the Kaiser-Franz charcoal-fired furnace in Eisenerz from 1848 to the plant's closure in 1901. Inv. No. 9.972

iron was produced in Roman times and the Middle Ages. Before it was installed in the Museum, this hearth was used in a successful smelting trial.

As temperatures of 'only' 1,200–1,300°C could be achieved using this method, the iron residue, known as a 'bloom', was a solid mass that had to be heated before being shaped (hence 'wrought' iron).

Increasing demand for iron in the high middle ages caused pig iron producers to 'relocate' away from ore deposits to watercourses whose power was harnessed by waterwheels to work bellows. The taller, more efficient smelting works were now called shaft furnaces.

These shaft furnaces produced malleable iron with a low carbon content – steel, by today's definition. Their biggest disadvantage was that operations had to be interrupted because, after each smelting, the large blooms had to be removed through an opening at the front of the furnace.

The melting point of iron is about 1,530°C, a temperature that was achievable after the 16th century through the use of stronger bellows, blast air preheating and by constructing furnaces with narrower cross sections, so-called flowing furnaces. As of the 18th century, charcoal-fired furnaces were superseded by free-standing coke-fired furnaces, first in England, then elsewhere. Operation of a blast furnace requires blast air and an air heater, a coking plant to produce coke from hard coal and a sintering plant for ore dressing and agglomeration.

The Museum has on display two historical blowers, an 1820s wooden box blower from Assling/Jesenice and a cylindrical blower with balancier cast in Mariazell in 1847, that was used in the Kaiser-Franz blast furnace in the town of Eisenerz. A large animated diagram illustrates the complex operation of a modern coke furnace. An alternative to the blast fur-

nace is provided by direct reduction processes such as the Corex©
process developed by VOEST-ALPINE Industrieanlagenbau. It is shown
here in model form and in a computer simulation.

Steel
Liquid pig iron from flowing and blast furnaces contains around 4 per
cent carbon; to be made into steel, it must undergo a process of decarburisation. This was first achieved by burning charcoal in a refining fire, but the amounts of pig iron produced were small. At the end of the 18th century, Englishman Henry Cort invented the puddling furnace that permitted the use of coal in the conversion of pig iron into wrought iron and increased production – a prerequisite for rolling the first rails. Through an aperture, a steelworker stirred the molten iron in the furnace ('puddling'); this resulted in the escape of carbon by oxidization. Puddling was eventually superseded by the Bessemer process, named after its inventor, Englishman Henry Bessemer. This was a technique that allowed air to be blown through molten pig iron at the bottom of a

Model of a refining hearth, Vienna, 1817. High-strength wrought iron manufactured using charcoal-fired pig iron could be produced only in such refining hearths until 1830/40. Inv. No. 9.869

Bessemer converter, Turrach, 1866. Thanks to his knowledge of England and his contacts there, Peter Tunner, on behalf of Prince Schwarzenberg, succeeded in opening Austria's first Bessemer converter in 1863. Inv. No. 9.508

pyriform converter, thus causing the oxygen to combine with the carbon present in the pig iron.

One of the first furnaces in Austria (Turrach) to utilize the Bessemer process is exhibited here. Built in 1866, it had a capacity of three tons.

The transition from puddling to the Bessemer process also marks the important advent of mechanisation and the application of science in steel production. The experienced puddler, a man who earned well but who had a physically demanding job, was replaced by chemists carrying spectroscopes and a number of skilled plant operators. In itself, this is a good example of the development of vocational qualifications as a result of technological change.

In 1864, the technology of mass steel production culminated in the introduction of the Siemens-Martin (open hearth) process that long held sway as the industry standard and which permitted large quantities of scrap to be melted down for the first time.

More recently, it has been superseded by the basic oxygen process (originally known as the Linz-Donawitz, or LD-process) as developed in Austria. To show that sheets of LD-steel were suitable for shipbuilding, VOEST constructed several seagoing freighters in the late 1950s. A large model of the 'Linzertor' is evidence of this period of transition.

High-grade steel-making accounts for around a third of world steel production of about 750 million tons. Since the early 20th century, it has utilized the electric-arc furnace as invented by the Frenchman Paul Héroult.

The section on electric steel-making is immediately followed by two related topics: the first one considers alloying elements that lend raw steel a number of exactly defined properties, and the second one examines secondary metallurgy, a smelting process that enhances the purity of high-grade steel.

The 1970s electro slag re-smelting furnace that is on display was used to produce high-purity steel for specialized applications such as piston rings or valves.

The section entitled 'Hard as Steel' looks beyond technology. Iron and steel are seen as durable, hard-wearing and tough, qualities that have resulted in their widespread figurative use in everyday life and in politics. On display is a rust-resistant steel helmet from 1913 that also represents the metaphorical use of metal, as does a World War II Iron Cross.

Non-Ferrous Metals

Owing to large ore deposits, iron and steel, the most important metals, have traditionally played an important role in Austrian society. For long periods, however, non-ferrous metal ores were also mined in the Eastern Alps and precious, non-ferrous, heavy and light metals were produced. Secondary production acquired a degree of importance in the late 20th century. For example, Brixlegg smelting plant in the Tyrol, where copper ores were smelted for centuries, has specialized in recovering copper from scrap metal. Nowadays around 40 per cent of the

Gold and silversmith's workshop, Vienna, 19th century. Table with five workstations and the tools needed to make a ring. Inv. No. 10.260

Wax head of a female bronze worker, Vienna, c. 1900. Using this wax head, the 'Gewerbe-hygienisches Museum', founded in the late 1880s, drew attention to the risks of working with heavy metals. Inv. No. 33.924

copper produced in the industrialized countries comes from recycling. After abandoning electrolysis, the smelting plant at Ranshofen in Upper Austria is now geared solely to the production of secondary aluminium from scrap.

Not far from the Austrian border, on territory that was formerly part of the Habsburg monarchy, lies the unusual deposit of Idrija in Slovenia. For 500-odd years, mercury was mined from cinnabar here and made Idrija the world's second-largest producer of this metal after Almadén in Spain.

The mining and processing of mercury, tin, zinc and lead were hazardous activities for humans and the environment alike. This is exemplified by the wax head, formerly in the collection of the 'Gewerbe-hygienisches Museum', of a female bronze worker exhibiting skin disease. The main source of information here is a listening station where visitors can listen on demand to reports on heavy metal poisoning written by Paracelsus, Egon Erwin Kisch and the safety inspectorate.

Smelting of gold and silver-bearing ores peaked in Austria as early as the 16th century. An exhibition at mezzanine level considers the mythical importance of precious metals. Gold, silver and platinum have always exerted a fascination on people and their importance in jewellery making and industrial applications, like the minting of coins, is highlighted. A reconstruction of an original goldsmith's workshop is on view.

Metalworking

When fashioning metals, a distinction is made between creative forming techniques and machining. In jointing, on the other hand, component parts are assembled together to form larger units. Original machines and tools, some of which can be demonstrated, as well as finished and semi-finished products, are on display here.

Decorative cast iron, Horschowitz/Hořovice and Blanz/Blansko, 1829–39. From left: Crown Prince Ferdinand, Kaiser Franz I, Venus, Bacchus, Rudolf Count Wrbna

Casting
The oldest and most important shaping technique is casting. For centuries, guns and church bells alike have been cast from iron, other metals and various alloys. In art, too, cast metal has had a host of uses – from jewellery to monumental bronzes. A sand casting core moulding shop has been dismantled to allow visitors to grasp the complexities of the casting process. Powder metallurgy is a modern variation of creative forming techniques.

Forging and Rolling
Forging, pressing, rolling and pulling are re-shaping techniques. Forging by the blacksmith at his anvil was the most important shaping technique for thousands of years. Water-driven hammers began to be used in the Middle Ages, and from the 19th century, the job was done by steam, hydraulic and pneumatic hammers and presses. Scotsman and resident of Vienna John Haswell constructed the world's first steam-hydraulic forging press in 1860/61. The oldest surviving specimen dates from 1872 and is on display in the 'Heavy Industry' exhibition. Unlike hammer forging that typified industrialization in the 19th century, screw

Forging press, Vienna, 1872. Scotsman John Haswell built the world's first steam-hydraulic forging press in 1860–61. It partly replaced existing forging hammers. Inv. No. 527

presses, with die-forging dies for precision parts, turbine blades for example, have remained important to this day.

In rolling, metal is shaped between rotating cylinders. Products with flat surfaces, smooth finishes or profiled cross sections are manufactured in this way. Since the Middle Ages, soft metals like lead have been rolled into thin strips, as has soft wrought iron since the 18th century. The great advantage of this method is that it guarantees consistent quality and large numbers, unlike forging. This is why rolling remains the most important forming technique for plates, rails and supports as well as for profiles. A model of an electric cogging mill from the early 20th century is shown in demonstration mode.

Wiredrawing can be regarded as a special type of rolling. Wire is one of the most important semi-finished products and is used in the manufacture of nails, chains, wire mesh and cables. Wire was at first drawn by hand: using pliers, the wiredrawer drew it through the holes of a drawplate, thereby reducing its diameter. Hydraulic and steam power were later used in this process. Wire with a diameter greater than five millimetres is rolled; thinner wire must as before be cold-drawn.

Heavy Industry 61

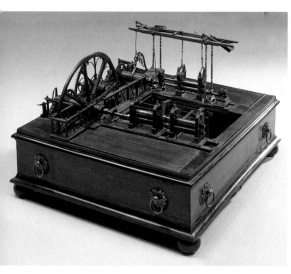

Model of a sheet-rolling mill, Hall in Tyrol, c. 1800. The advent of rolling mills allowed the industrial manufacture of sheet metal, rails and girders. Inv. No. 9.778

Turning, Milling, Drilling

Metallic workpieces usually acquire their final form by having their surfaces machined. Wherever metallic swarf is found, a cutting operation has been in progress. Cutting methods include turning, milling and drilling as well as sawing, planing, filing and grinding. The principle is always the same: a very hard cutting edge is applied to a softer workpiece from which material (swarf) is removed. Without machining, there would be no products with close-fitting moving parts such as sewing machines, bicycles or cars.

Metal turning is closely related to woodturning. The workpiece is mounted, rotated and worked with a tool. The lathe tool was originally held in the hand, but after about 1800 was mounted in a support that allowed machine parts with straight, clean lines to be made. The collection of original machine tools on display here ranges from a wooden manual lathe from 1840 to a new, ready-to-use CNC-controlled lathe from the 1990s. These exhibits illustrate not only the development of machine tools but also the changing demands made on their operators.

Riveting and Welding

Besides the shaping of metal, jointing techniques are also very important in the manufacture of industrial products. Jointing means the creation of permanent connections between workpieces. Joints made using nails, clamps or screws can usually be undone with no material damage. Permanent joints made using rivets, welding, soldering or bonding, on the other hand, cannot be undone without material destruction. For almost a century after the 1840s riveting was the most widely used jointing technique in iron and steel construction. Ships, locomotives, steam boilers, bridges and halls (such as the Museum's) were held together by countless numbers of rivets. Two and a half million of them were used in the construction of the Eiffel Tower in 1887–89, and almost eight million were used to build the Forth Bridge in Scotland, built 1883–90. Dating from 1891, the rack railway steam locomotive of the Vordernberg-Eisenerz ore mine and its boiler are examples of the use of riveting techniques in locomotive construction. Welding gradually

Machine tools, 19th and 20th century. This display of lathes, milling and drilling machines since 1840 reveals both technical developments and changing demands on those who used them

began to supersede riveting at the beginning of the 20th century and remains the most important method of creating permanent joints.

Two related topics – 'The Riveter's Strength' and 'The Welder's Art' – consider the vocational qualifications of these skilled workers.

Leading Sector Steel

Iron and steel are still by far the most important metals in the world in terms of volume, and are the main focus of this exhibition. On entering the 'Heavy Industry' exhibition from the Central Hall, visitors first notice the display of original machinery. After World War II and pilot tests in Germany and Switzerland, Voest's Linz smelting plant succeeded in introducing a new method of steel-making known as the Linz-Donawitz process that takes its name from the locations in Upper Austria and in

Styria where it was first applied in 1952/53. Today, around two thirds of the world's steel is smelted using the LD-process, better known in English as the basic oxygen process (BOP), in which molten pig iron in the crucible is refined into steel by the high-speed injection of pure oxygen. Up to 300 tons of pig iron can be 'blown' into steel in about 20 minutes using this method. The exhibits, a 1952 30-ton LD-crucible with a scrap chute, slag pan, four ingot moulds and a steel ingot, not only reconstruct early 1950s technology, but also give visitors some idea of the dimensions and materials associated with heavy industry. A walk along the raised catwalk further deepens visitors' impressions. A working model of the hall illustrates the complete cycle from pig iron mixing to ingot casting. A 3-D computer simulation at a control console illustrates the technology of the new BOP steel works that opened at Donawitz in 2000. Twice a day, a sound installation gives visitors some idea of the noise levels in a steel works.

After walking round the exhibits, visitors can read about the political and economic aspects of heavy industry in the 20th century in 'The Era of Steel'; social aspects are considered in 'Working at the Steel Mill'. These two exhibitions are arranged around a model of the 'Hermann Göring' steelworks that was built in Linz during World War II. Planned at the drawing board as an integrated steelworks and realized on a greenfield site, it employed more than 20,000 people at its height.

   A set of regulations from 1886 from the Zeltweg iron and steel works of the 'Alpine Montangesellschaft' shows just how rigidly discipline was at first maintained in factories, from starting work to being dismissed.

Locomotive boiler, Vienna, 1890, from locomotive 97.201 on the Erzberg rack railway. A typical product of heavy industry in the 19th century. Inv. No. 50.395/2

Blast-furnace worker, Donawitz steel works, c. 1950. This branch of heavy industry was a leading sector of industrialization both in terms of its technology and commitment to its workforce

Steelwork is heavy manual work but it is also highly skilled work, which is why it was always important for steel companies to retain their workers. This they did by providing fringe benefits, as shown in a series of photographs of the showers at Böhler in Düsseldorf, the dental clinic at Voest's Linz foundry, the Catholic works chaplaincy established in 1953, again at Voest in Linz, the works sports club, 'SK Voest' (Austrian football champions in 1974), the Voest spa at Lake Weikerl near Linz and a detached family house in a Voest-run housing estate in Traun near Linz. Excerpts from interviews in the 1980s with steelworkers talking about their shift work and occupational accidents can be heard on demand at a listening seat.

   The iron and steel industry was a leading sector of industrialization and remained so until the post-war boom of the 1950s and 1960s. The coal industry was the first to experience a crisis, followed by the steel industry. In Upper Styria, at one time a heavily industrialized region, things were turned upside down. The factories that did not close had to cut their workforces drastically, but are now able to survive by specializing in high-value finishing work. This is acknowledged here with a number of exhibits ranging from the ESU process in secondary metallurgy, turbine blades for a gas-fired power station forged between dies, the profile of a 120-metre-long head-hardened high-speed rail and the laser-welded mill bar of a door for a lightweight car body.

LaH

Energy

Energy

Converter chain. Inv. No. 50.866

Energy plays a central role in the appliances we use in our everyday lives. Although we are hardly aware of the fact, every time we operate a vehicle, a kitchen appliance or a means of communication, the use of energy is involved. The Museum's 'Energy' exhibition illustrates the various aspects of the conversion and the use of energy.

The use of energy in history is associated with shortages of energy sources, so-called 'energy crises'. Preventive measures such as rationalization and 'energy saving' are the hallmarks of such shortages. Periods of wealth, economic recovery and population growth, on the other hand, are often associated with new energy sources, conversion processes and methods of use.

The Museum's 'Energy' exhibition looks at the 'Production', 'Distribution' and 'Consumption' of energy. In terms of physics, however, it is incorrect to talk about the 'production' of energy; 'supply' is more appropriate. Energy is neither 'produced' nor 'consumed'.

Coming from the Central Hall, visitors first see a large-scale experiment, the so-called converter chain. By turning a handle 90 times, visitors pump water into a higher basin. The potential energy gained in this way is then converted into other types of energy in a highly visual and effective demonstration. After eleven or so minutes, the 'conversion losses' cause the machine to come to a stop because the available energy has been converted into non-usable low temperature heat.

The central Forum gives access to the 'Energy' exhibition that is divided into three sections illustrating the supply, transport and use of energy throughout history.

The Era of the Arts

'The Era of the Arts' covers the period from the dawn of history to the beginnings of industrialization. Energy during this time was used in close proximity to its source. Even in antiquity, the utilization and amplification of power were referred to as the 'mechanical arts'. In the Middle Ages and in the early modern era, craftsmen with an understanding of the mechanical arts were known as 'Kunstmeister'. They constructed water supply and pumping stations, hydraulic engines and muscle-powered machines. The abbot of Stift Göttweig in Lower Austria had Salzburg's master carpenter Abraham Hueber build a hoist and a piped water supply to the monastery.

The Sun has always been an important source of energy. For as long as man was unable to make fire, solar energy was his only source of heat and light.

To perform physical work, men for centuries depended on their own brawn and the strength of animals. An individual was able to carry only small loads. If larger loads had to be moved or lifted, they had to be of a nature that allowed several people to lend a hand. Devices that amplified force brought some relief, certainly; it was thought that their use

Model of the installation of the obelisk in St Peter's Square in Rome. Inv. No. 50.882

outwitted nature! In the third century BC, the Greek mathematician and inventor Archimedes studied the functions of levers, wedges (inclined planes) and pulleys. In his law of equilibrium, he observed that the effort multiplied by the length of the effort arm equals the load multiplied by the length of the load arm. Let L be the load, E the effort, e the effort arm and w the load arm. Expressed as a mathematical formula, this is $E \times e = L \times w$. Visitors can gain first-hand experience of these mechanical principles in experiments using levers, wedges and pulleys. Other important mechanical aids were thrust screws and winches with which presses could be operated or loads lifted. The treadmill was an effective invention for lifting loads and drawing water. On a treadmill with outside steps, a man walking them at axle height was able to make full use of his body weight.

Animals were also used to power tread wheels, but were used mainly to drive gins and for transport. For long periods, heavy loads were hauled by horses – to the great detriment of their health. The yoke devised for oxen did not suit the build of horses because it compressed their windpipe, a problem that was solved by the invention of the horse collar, which spread the load onto the breast and shoulders.

   An example of how animal and man power can be utilized to move and lift great loads is shown in a model of the operation to shift an almost 26-metre-high obelisk into the centre of St Peter's Square in Rome, as required of master builder and architect Domenico Fontana by pope Sixtus V in 1586. Its ingenious position and the co-ordination of hundreds of men and animals give some indication of the difficulties involved in the undertaking.

By exploiting water and wind power, man was able to overcome his limited muscular power. To make best use of water and its flow rate, there are basically two types of waterwheels – those with vertical shafts and those with horizontal shafts. Among the latter type are counted overshot, middle-shot and undershot waterwheels.

A waterwheel with a vertical shaft usually has slightly inclined vanes, similar to today's Kaplan blades, and a wooden headrace that directs the water onto the vanes. With the aid of such simple mills, the force of

19th-century bucket mill. Inv. No. 708

water with small flow rates and high heads could be used to about 15 per cent efficiency. With millstones driven by a vertical shaft and the lack of a drive mechanism suggest that this is the oldest mill of its type.

The first written records of undershot mill wheels, which achieved efficiencies of around 35 per cent, date from the first century BC. The basic advantage of such mills was that rivers or streams did not need to be diverted to operate them. An unusual type of undershot mill was the ship mill: lying in the course of a river, it was a ship with mill wheels attached by ropes.

In Central Europe, the first overshot mill wheels appeared in the 14th century. Making use of kinetic energy and the weight of the water bearing down on their wheel from above, they achieved efficiencies of up to 75 per cent, but they also required steeper heads and for that reason were found mainly in mountainous areas. Visitors can experiment with an undershot and an overshot wheel and see how each differs in efficiency. On display is a model of a 30-km-long stretch of the river Traisen in Lower Austria on which 69 mills were located; it illustrates just how intensively water-power was used in Austria around 1850.

The Era of Power Stations

'The Era of Power Stations' covers the period of industrialization to the beginning of the 20th century. Power continued to be generated near its consumers and power stations supplied individual factories or localized areas with gas or electricity.

Until the beginning of the 18th century, only physical strength, water and wind power were available to provide mechanical energy. With the aid of steam engines, it now became possible to convert the chemical

Carboniferous swamp (tempera). Inv. No. 39.974

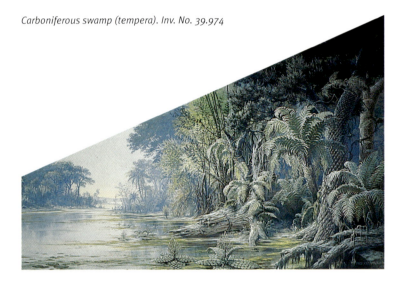

energy of coal into mechanical energy. Starting in Britain, industrialization was made possible and accelerated by, among other things, the supply and this new use of the energy stored in coal.

A tempera painting done at the time the Museum was founded shows a swamp forest with seed ferns, horsetails and lycopsids, vegetation typical of the Carboniferous Period, about 300 million years ago. It was a period of intensive coal formation.

Efficient steam boilers were needed for the construction of steam engines. After 1800 or so, the steam power of conventional cylindrical boilers no longer sufficed for the new type of steam engine. To increase the heating area, and thus also output, water-filled tubes were led through the combustion chamber. After 1840, the German doctor and inventor Ernst Alban worked on water tube boilers that were able to withstand steam pressure up to ten bar. Water partly evaporated in their slightly inclined tubes. Via two upright chambers, the water-and-steam mixture flowed into higher drums where the steam and water were separated.

Steam engines capable of operating pumps to remove water from mines were first built in the 18th century. In 1712, Thomas Newcomen, together with Thomas Savery, succeeded in constructing the first working atmospheric steam engine. It was Savery's suggestion to separate steam generation and steam use, and Newcomen applied it to Denis Papin's moving piston (Papin was the man who invented the pressure cooker in 1681). A layer of water above the piston solved the problem of sealing it.

Although steam engines were still inefficient, they rapidly found widespread use because they were mobile. Around 1770, some 100 steam engines were in use in the north of England. In 1722, Joseph Emanuel

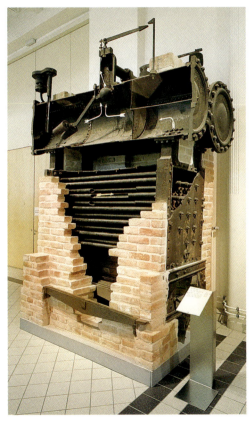

Ernst Alban's water-tube boiler. Inv. No. 829

Fischer von Erlach, with the help of the English engineer Isaac Potter, installed Austria's first atmospheric steam engine in the garden of Vienna's Schwarzenberg Palace. The original model of an atmospheric steam engine that Fischer von Erlach had built in 1732 before constructing his second steam engine is on display in the exhibition.

The Scottish instrument repairer James Watt is still widely regarded as the inventor of the steam engine, however. While repairing a model of a

Newcomen steam engine at Glasgow University, Watt was able to study how it functioned and pinpoint its weaknesses. Crucial to the success of Watt's steam engine was his realization that it should comprise three parts. In 1765, he built a pilot model with a steam boiler, a cylinder enclosing the working piston and, most importantly, a separate condenser. His invention was patented in 1769 with the help of mine owner John Reobuck, but only the financial support of a new partner, Matthew Boulton, allowed Watt in 1776 to build the first steam engines to his design and to market them successfully.

The engines displayed here are still in working order. They start with one built in 1825 by Johann Fichtner; like Watt's, it is a beam steam engine.

Gallery of Steam Engines

When Watt's patent expired in 1800, other engineers tried to construct a more compact machine and to avoid the energy-consuming diversion of power by means of a beam. In the second half of the 19th century and at the beginning of the 20th century, engineers focused their efforts on developing fast-running engines with horizontal cylinders. In 1882, Thomas Alva Edison was one of the first to use such engines to power dynamos in New York City's first public power station. A high number of revolutions was required because the steam engines and dynamos were directly connected without a gear unit. The reversal of the direction of rotation of steam engines – a prerequisite for their use in locomotives, steam ships and rolling mills – was made possible by the reversing gear as invented by George Stephenson, the English inventor of the railway locomotive. In the 19th century, steam-powered means of transport ushered in a new era of mobility: for the first time ever, large numbers of people and goods could be moved at speed.

Kaplan turbine. Inv. No. 16.776

Private and state schools of technology were established in the 19th century to train technical experts. Some of these institutions were later recognized as technological universities with the right to award doctorates in engineering.

In 1895, Austrian Victor Kaplan began his mechanical engineering studies at Vienna University of Technology (founded in 1815 as the Polytechnic Institute). The area given over to the engineering profession is modelled on the laboratory where in 1912 Kaplan developed the turbine that now bears his name. On display is the world's first turbine that was used in Velm, near Vienna, in 1919; original pilot models and facsimiles of the patent specifications are also on show.

Kaplan's example illustrates how technological developments are not only the result of creativity and an inventive mind, but also rely on lengthy and labour-intensive series of experiments. Whether or not a product is successful often becomes apparent only decades later. Success depends not only on the quality of the invention but also on the prevailing social and economic conditions. A related exhibition called 'Success and Failure' contains exhibits of some inventions that have and have not been a success. For instance, the electric motors devised by Martin Egger and Johann Kravogl worked but they were not powerful enough.

In 1889, Carl de Laval's steam turbine satisfied the demands of the day and he immediately developed the right technical solution. Jean Lenoir's gas engine, on the other hand, enjoyed only a few decades of success, while its principle, that of the internal combustion engine, is used to this day. At the end of the 19th century, inventor Thomas Alva Edison used clever marketing to further the success of his electrical products.

By the end of the 19th century, a number of prime movers had been developed for goods manufacturing. Steam engines or water turbines may have been suitable for use in factories, but for small businesses

Electric machines by Martin Egger, Johann Kravogl, Felix Wankel and Julius Hock

they were out of the question because they were both too expensive and too complicated to use. Despite initial successes, even the internal combustion engines that were developed after the 1860s were unable to meet tradesmen's requirements: low running costs, high output, irregular loads and frequent stopping and starting. Only with the advent of electric motors did small businesses have suitable power sources at their disposal. Around 1900, they were regarded as the 'saviours of the small business'.

Electric drives and generators had been developed on the basis of scientific discoveries during the 18th and 19th centuries. In 1819, the Danish physicist and chemist Hans Christian Ørsted discovered that electric current can deflect a compass needle. In 1820, the French physicist and mathematician André Marie Ampère discovered that two live conductors are attracted to each other. The English physicist and chemist Michael Faraday was finally able in 1831 to explain both effects in a comprehen-

Alternating-current generator by the Compagnie l'Alliance. Inv. No. 4.982

sive theory and furnished proof of electromagnetic induction, i.e. the occurrence of voltage in a coil moving through a magnetic field. These discoveries found practical application in the first effective electric generator that was devised by the Frenchman Hyppolyte Pixii in 1832. Electric generators are used in energy conversion: dynamos convert mechanical energy into electric energy, while electric motors convert electric energy into mechanical energy. One of the Museum's oldest alternating-current generators was built in 1870 by the Compagnie L'Alliance. It has a 2 kW output and its rotor coils revolve in a field of steel horseshoe magnets. The Imperial and Royal Austrian Army used the generator to illuminate battle areas.

The 19th century public was shown the latest manufactured goods, including engines, at regional and international exhibitions. These fairs

This display is modelled on a 19th-century industrial exhibition

were modelled on a number of spectacular world exhibitions that were tailored to the tastes of the middle classes and attracted millions of visitors. Organized by government bodies and trade and industry associations, such shows allowed countries to present themselves to the world, but they were also intended to promote trade and industry and to enable visitors to compare products.

As Europe's industrial cities grew rapidly in the 19th century, so too did their traffic and communications infrastructures as well as the networks supplying them with water, light and power. Gaslight turned night into day and provided street lighting for everyone. By the end of the 19th century, gaslight and electric light were rivals. In 1891, the Austrian

Energy 77

chemist Carl Auer von Welsbach (1858–1929) invented incandescent gaslight by impregnating the gas mantle with metal oxides that glowed in the flame. The same amount of gas now produced a far brighter light. 'Auer's lights' could also burn gas from coking plants that in conventional gaslights did not burn brightly enough.

Viennese Gas Streetlamp.
Inv. No. 17.233

Electrification began in Austria in 1886 when the country's first municipal power plant was put into service in Scheibbs (Lower Austria). Vienna's first electric tram carried passengers in 1897 and at the start of the 20th century, gaslights were gradually replaced by electric lighting. Electric motors were also used for the first time in farming during the inter-war years. For reasons of cost and to allow farmers to use electric motors wherever they were needed, they were mounted in baskets or wheelbarrows.

Energy requirements grew steadily as industrialization progressed and they were met by gas or electricity. The main advantage of these energy sources was that in supply networks they could be moved over large distances without great losses; they were also suitable for a wide range of applications. Gasworks had supplied municipal gas consumers since the start of the 19th century. The first electric power stations followed towards the end of that century. Power stations were originally almost all run by private companies, but were soon largely taken over by municipal authorities because, on the one hand, private gas suppliers put profit before quality assurance and security of supply, and, on the other, the serious investment needed to set up electricity supply chains could only be found by municipal or nationalized companies.

Although the steam engine came to symbolize the process of industrialization, in areas with a plentiful supply of water it was unable to compete with the waterwheel or the technically superior water turbine which could be used directly in production and which had been used to produce electricity economically since the end of the 19th century. Having called for the development of a new water-powered engine, the 'French Society for the Encouragement of Industry' in 1827 awarded Benoit Fourneyron its prize for his inward-flowing radial turbine that was easily regulated and achieved efficiencies of almost 80 per cent. In 1838, the American Samuel Howd received a patent for his outward-flowing radial turbine that was significantly improved by his fellow American James Bicheno Francis. To take advantage of high heads with

The interior of the machine units at Ruetz power station: the generator. Inv. No. 39.035

low water flow rates, the American engineer Lester Allan Pelton developed the Pelton wheel in 1880. In 1912, the Austrian Victor Kaplan invented a propeller turbine for large flows at low heads; it now bears his name. When Austria lost the rich coalfields of Silesia, Bohemia and Moravia in the aftermath of World War I, the country made greater use of waterpower. Output from its hydroelectric plants doubled between 1918 and 1929. One of the two turbines from Ruetz power station that went on stream in 1912 to power the Mittenwald railway in Tyrol is the largest 'walk-in' exhibit in the Museum's 'Energy' exhibition.

Reconstruction of the Milles workshop powered by transmission. Inv. No. 60.226

The interior of the machine units at Ruetz power station: a turbine.
Inv. No. 39.035

THE ERA OF NETWORKS

'The Era of Networks' examines the 20th century when energy was delivered from its place of 'production' via networked systems such as pipelines or electric cables to – usually distant – locations where it was 'consumed'.

The search for new sources of energy was prompted both by increases in the price of coal at the beginning of the 20th century and awareness that coal resources were finite as much as by the steady growth in the demand for energy for manufacturing, services and travel. At first oil, then gas and uranium, came into use alongside the long-established energy sources of waterpower and coal. Electric current became increasingly important as a source of secondary and end energy. Like coal, the fossil fuels oil and gas are also finite resources whose conversion and use releases harmful substances into the environment.

Around the middle of the 20th century, the use of nuclear energy appeared to provide an answer, but the radioactivity that is released in nuclear fission itself gave rise to new problems. There were thus more calls for the use of renewable energy sources like solar and wind power or biomass.

As use of these new energy sources increased, they were increasingly converted and processed in large-scale plants. This sometimes meant that Utopian-sounding projects were planned and even realized. The engineer's dream of the huge Itaipú hydroelectric plant on the border between Brazil and Paraguay became reality, for instance.

The infrastructure needed for the supply and use of energy grew in the 20th century to a previously unimagined scale. Extensive networks, some even with a global span, were built to provide electricity and communication services and networks of petrol stations were created to supply petroleum products.

Petroleum, a mixture of various hydrocarbons, and natural gas, with methane as its main constituent, were formed over the course of millions of years from the decomposition of organic matter. The oil industry began to develop with the first oil drilling in the United States in 1859. Thanks to the widespread use of oil lamps and, later, of internal combustion engines, there was a sharp increase in the demand for oil in the second half of the 19th century.

At the beginning of the 1860s, rich oil deposits were discovered in Galicia. Around 1910, they made Austria-Hungary the world's third largest oil producer behind the United States and Russia. In Austria today, commercially important oilfields are found mainly in the Vienna Basin. Natural gas was first discovered in Austria in 1891 at Wels in Upper Austria. It too has been an important factor in the world economy since World War II.

Petroleum and natural gas meet about two thirds of total energy consumption in Austria and are thus the country's most important sources of energy.

Using original objects and models, diagrams and films, the exhibition illustrates the formation of hydrocarbon deposits, their detection by geological exploration and their recovery by drilling and the sinking of oil wells. In addition, the exhibition looks at the construction of pipelines and the temporary storage of natural gas in depleted oil and gas fields.

Petroleum cannot be used in its raw state. Before it can be used as petrol (gasoline), fuel oil, lubricant or a raw material for the chemical industry, it must first be distilled, desulphurized and refined in an oil refinery before it is admixed to other products. An exhibit and a computer game explain the complex processes involved.

The huge dependency of many economies on the cheap availability of petroleum and natural gas is a cause of conflict as countries battle over their share of these resources. The production and transport of over 3.5 billion tons of oil a year is not possible without causing serious environmental problems. The large-scale combustion of fossil fuels is also the cause of increased levels of carbon dioxide in the Earth's atmosphere. The resultant climate change poses a threat to the planet's ecosystems on a hitherto unknown scale.

To meet the demand for electricity in industrialized countries, different types of generating plants are needed. Depending on their size and type, each gives rise to problems of its own. In Austria, electrical power is produced mainly using water and fossil fuels. Conversion into electricity takes place in about 1,750 run-of-river stations, 110 storage power stations and 210 thermal electric power stations. In addition, wind farms and solar plants are used in power generation. A number of

Model of Galgenbichel power station. Inv. No. 50.932

experiments, models and charts explain the main types of power station used in Austria today.

Thermal power stations mainly burn fossil fuels (coal, gas, oil). Steam or gas turbines convert the thermal energy that is produced into kinetic energy from which electrical energy is produced with the help of generators. To increase efficiency, co-generation plants were developed that besides the electricity produced also use waste heat as heating or as process heat. On display is a model of the Donaustadt (Block 3) thermal power plant, Austria's most up-to-date co-generation plant.

In storage power stations, the potential energy of water is converted by means of kinetic energy into electric energy: water from a reservoir flows through pipes to the power station where it drives a turbine that in turn produces electric power with the help of a generator. Francis or Pelton turbines are usually used in storage power stations. By different means, pump storage stations convert surplus electric energy into the potential energy of water. A four-machine unit consists of a turbine, generator, pump and motor, while a two-machine unit is equipped with a pump turbine and a motor generator. Senior pupils in the Carinthian town of Malta built the model of Galgenbichel power station that is on display. It has two sets of pump turbines and is one of Austria's most efficient power stations.

In the 1950s and 60s, Austria, too, decided to harness the peaceful use of nuclear energy whose use was to be promoted by a national nuclear programme that included a research reactor at Seibersdorf near Vienna. In 1956, the headquarters of the International Atomic Energy Agency for the Promotion of the Civilian Use of Nuclear Energy was established in Vienna. Construction work on Austria's first nuclear power station began in 1972 at Zwentendorf in Lower Austria. Because of strong opposition to it from some sections of society, a plebiscite was held in 1978 that resulted in a majority vote against nuclear energy. Zwentendorf never produced any electricity.

The extensive network that supplies our electricity has profoundly affected every aspect of our lives. As it does not make economic sense to store electricity, complex technical installations are required if full use is to be made of its advantages – easy availability, small losses while it is transported to consumers, a wide variety of applications and good controllability. Power must be generated when it is needed. As the use and availability of electricity increased, dependence on it as an energy source also grew.

Electric power reaches consumers through a distribution system of overhead electric cables and transformer stations. 'From the Power Station to the Plug' is a collection of models and original exhibits that shows how electricity is fed into a typical network. Power stations generate electricity with a voltage up to 27 kilovolts. To reduce losses, high voltages of up to 400 kilovolts are transmitted along electric cables. The live elements of high-voltage plants must be isolated at great expense.

Near centres of consumption, high-voltage current is transformed to medium voltage current between 10 and 30 kilovolts. This is the level used by trams, underground systems, and trade and industry. For domestic consumers, small businesses and agriculture, the voltage is further reduced in transformer substations to 230/400 volts.

As the demand for electricity varies constantly, problems can arise in the national grid caused either by a lack or an excess of power. Load

Power dispatcher game. Inv. No. 50.947

dispatchers coordinate the production and distribution of electricity to meet demand for power at any given time and to make optimum use of different types of power station. Electricity consumption varies both throughout the day and throughout the year. The daily demand for electricity is illustrated in diagrams known as load curves. Generally, the power industry differentiates between base, average and peak loads. The base load satisfies the demand for the share of electricity that is always required. Austria's base load is generated mainly using run-of-river stations. The peak load occurs when demand for electricity on any given day is at its greatest. This share of electricity is generated by gas turbine and storage power stations that can be switched on and off quickly.

A load distribution game allows visitors to supply Austria's power needs for a day using various types of power station.

Exhibition Mine

To meet the steadily growing demand for coal for domestic use and as a source of power for steam engines and steam turbines, mining methods had to be constantly improved. At the beginning of the 20th century, a reconstruction of the Gabriele mine in Karwin, then in Austrian Silesia, was built in the Museum's basement. Among other things, square set wooden supports, extraction using a pneumatic drilling machine and a coal cutter as well as coal transport using a shaker conveyor and mine cars are shown. In 1954, modern steel supports were added to the mine reconstruction and, as part of the re-installation of the 'Energy' exhibition in 1999, a drum cutter-loader and a tunnelling machine from the 1970s were added.

Chain conveyor with mine cars

High-Voltage Room

Electrical discharges like lightning and St. Elmo's fire that surrounds ships during a thunderstorm have always fascinated humans. Both for research and teaching purposes, but also for fun, scientists have built machines that produce artificial lightning. Lightning is caused by the separation of electric charge into positive and negative charge carriers, which in turn gives rise to electric tension. When it is discharged, sound effects and luminous phenomena occur that we know as thunder and lightning.

Van-de-Graaff generator
Inv. No. 50.939

In the Museum's high-voltage room, demonstrations are given using a Van de Graaff generator and a Tesla coil; they are surrounded by a Faraday cage that shields them from external electrical fields.

The Tesla coil was devised by Nikola Tesla (1856–1943) for power transmission. Tesla was a Croatian physicist and electrical engineer who studied at Graz University of Technology. In 1882 he moved to Paris to work for Continental Edison. A year later, he built the first induction motor. In 1884, Edison called him to the United States to work as his research assistant, but differences of opinion about alternating current and direct current systems soon caused them to part company. Tesla was a specialist in high-frequency engineering and in his own laboratory developed remote-control systems for boats and high-frequency coils for radio and television transmission.
VoA/TrM

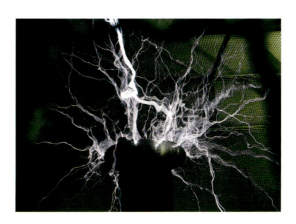

Tesla transformer.
Inv. No. 50.940

Mass Production – Luxury Goods

Mass Production – Luxury Goods

Technology and design from the Biedermeier era to the Vienna World Exhibition 1804–1873

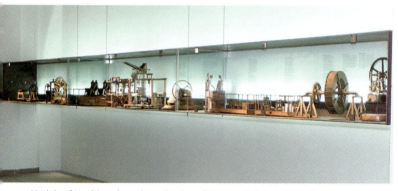

Models of Machines from the collection of Vienna's Polytechnic Institute

The Exhibition

The exhibition entitled 'Mass Production – Luxury Goods' represents one of the core collections in the Technisches Museum Wien, that of the so-called 'Fabriksprodukten-Kabinett' (Collection of Manufactured Products) as founded by Emperor Franz I. Crowned Emperor of Austria in 1804, he called on his dominions in 1807 to send him manufactured goods that would give him an idea of the industriousness of the Habsburg monarchy's craftsmen and their products. Taking the Biedermeier period as its focus, the imperial collection became one of the most significant and extensive of 19th century collections. There was nothing that was not collected from the three realms of nature – animal, vegetable and mineral; semi-finished and finished goods were also collected. To make them more widely known, parts of this 'Collection of Manufactured Products' are now on public display in the Technisches Museum Wien for the first time.

The Concept

The layout of the exhibition has been determined by the gallery's location at the west end of the first floor, located above the Heavy Industry display. Its main attraction is a 120-ton steel converter that projects into the exhibition; it had to be integrated into a space containing Biedermeier objects that very often are delicate in nature. The display cases were arranged along strictly symmetrical lines. Originally, the collection was arranged according to materials and production technologies; this has been abandoned in favour of a themed narrative. Corresponding pairs of concepts now define the exhibition's six main chapters: 'Nature and Culture', 'Idyll and Upheaval', 'Surface and Substance', 'Need and Luxury', 'Original and Series' plus 'Centre and Periphery'. These key chapters are presented within large steel frames that support the display cases and at the same time tie in with the Heavy Industry exhibition below.

Dedicated to the founders of the exhibition, Franz and Ferdinand, a double display case at the entrance has the shape of an abstract double eagle, the symbol of the Habsburg monarchy. In parallel to the main narrative strand, models of agricultural and other machines are presented in display cases hanging from thin steel wires that form a suspended counterpoint to the massive steel elements. At the end of the tour, paper and textile pattern books illustrate Goethe's theory of colour.

Around The Exhibition

Prologue

Where one of the loveliest and most extensive collections from the Biedermeier era is concerned, the Habsburg ruler Franz I is unavoidable. He was, after all, the man responsible for establishing it. A number of particularly attractive or novel pieces were dedicated to Emperor Franz and the crown prince and future emperor Ferdinand: portraits and busts, for instance, but also everyday items bearing the double eagle are united here. They form a microcosm of the sheer breadth of this vast collection. Showpieces made of cut and polished glass predominate here, although even the makers of brushes, combs and glass beads as

Double eagle made of glass beads and pins. Inv. No. 62.240

Döberein table lighter. Inv. No. 19.374

well as ivory carvers paid homage to their Emperor and demonstrated their artistry. Whether Bohemia, Hungary, Lower and Upper Austria or Venice, the various parts of the Habsburg monarchy are represented here. In other words, these select items also symbolize what was once a huge, multi-ethnic state.

Nature and Culture

Including the four classic natural substances horn, tortoiseshell, ivory and mother-of-pearl, nature offers a wealth of material that mankind has utilised over time. Unlike its 'exotic relations', horn was genuinely a mass product article in Europe's agrarian societies. Yet nature also came up with far more complex systems, such as natural dyes, for instance: madder and carmine, the most precious dye by far, the very epitome of luxury.

The 19th century dedicated itself to studying, systematizing and explaining nature. In 1868, for instance, scientists succeeded in unravelling the chemical composition of the madder used in Turkey red colouring and produced the dye alizarin. The world's first 'synthetic' material, celluloid, was invented almost at the same time. This substitute was badly needed to satisfy the demand for billiard balls in the saloons of the American West, as narwhal tusk and ivory were no longer able to satisfy the burgeoning demand. Thus another step was taken in lessening dependence on natural materials.

Idyll and Upheaval

The Biedermeier era is characterized by withdrawal into the private sphere. The cults of friendship and remembrance, penmanship, treasuring locks and ornaments of hair, circles of friends and salons, parlour games, outings to the country, walks and strolls in the open air all testify to the yearning for some kind of idyll far removed from political and social upheaval. The idyll was obviously fractured and another, harsh reality was about to descend upon it: rapid technological change, social tension and increased political repression. In short, beneath its calm surface, the Biedermeier era was in a state of ferment. There was no stopping the Industrial Revolution. As symbols of industrialization, the steam engine and particularly the textile industry represented the emergence of the age of industry and mass production. Following the hiatus of the 1848 Revolution, the process of industrialization culminated initially during the 'Gründerzeit', a period of strong economic growth that began some years before the Vienna World Exhibition of 1873.

Surface and Substance

Surface and substance: a bewildering play of appearance and reality, of inside and outside, of imitation and irritation. The protagonists in this game were materials and manufacturing methods, some of which were wholly new. Substitutes and imitations simulated more noble surfaces. This applied as much to silver plating as artificial marble, marbled paper, wafer-thin veneers or paper made with wood pulp.

The gleaming, black surface of Hyalith glass is confusing because the impenetrable, lacquered-looking surface of these 'stone' glasses does not allow us to see through them. Cased and opaque twist glass, in contrast, offer new insights altogether. The foreground and background begin to dissolve. Where does the surface start? Where does the substance end? The 'windows' in the cased glass eventually become 'lenses' that deceive the penetrating gaze in various ways. Microscope lenses provide far more detailed insights into matter, of course.

Jugs and a bowl made of spun glass. Inv. Nos. 11.802, 19.388, 19.387

The Theory of Colour

The foundations of modern design were laid during the Biedermeier era. Textile, paper and wallpaper patterns sometimes reveal a striking degree of modernity: iris stalks, lightning flashes, strong colours full of contrasts – 200 years ago! There is a direct link between such modern design and technological developments in printing and dyeing at the outset of the Industrial Revolution.

A paper collar and paper patterns

Beyond the realm of technology, however, the development of early design was enormously influenced by one of the era's most visual individuals: Johann Wolfgang von Goethe. Thanks to his *Theory of Colour,* the designers of the day had at their disposal a set of aesthetic principles that allowed them to devise the most imaginative colour combinations. After the mid-1830s, the newly elaborated design repertoire fused with old patterns to form a gentler sort of modernity.

Need and Luxury

What are basic necessities? What are luxuries? These questions are a matter of perspective. What are unattainable luxuries for some can long since have become essential requirements for others. What satisfies the basic needs of some satisfies the need for consumption for pleasure's sake in others. Much of what was once considered to be a luxury, such as coffee or sugar, had long since become a basic necessity for people during the Biedermeier era and had become part of the bourgeois lifestyle. All that remained for the lower social classes to do was to imitate those above them by turning to substitutes such as chicory or fir coffee, cheap rum or inexpensive crockery.

In contrast to Baroque and Rococo opulence, however, Biedermeier luxury was characterized by moderation. Plain and honest ruled the day rather than the Baroque art of extravagance. Biedermeier man's desire for simplicity and health even led to a renewal of interest in hygiene, prompting people to bathe again! Wellbeing and physical cleanliness had become a civic need, a civic duty even.

Originals and Series

As industrialization progressed, technological developments and commercial thinking brought mass production to the fore. Replaceability and large quantities were the requirements. Standardized series products such as threaded screws, produced in the millions, became cheap mass products. Other technologies for the manufacture of standardized objects were created. If metal had until then been forged exclusively by hand, it was now cast iron and extruded products that moved into the salons of the bourgeoisie. Where glass had been exclusively hand-blown and cut before, now any number of items could be produced in the form of moulded glass. The shift from unique piece to mass-produced goods is the shift from craftwork to industrial production. Craftwork nevertheless survived in niche markets: besides millions of mechanically manufactured pencils, there were expensive and unique pieces such as glass fountain pens; hand-blown and hand-painted glass eyes kept their share of the market alongside mass-produced spectacle frames.

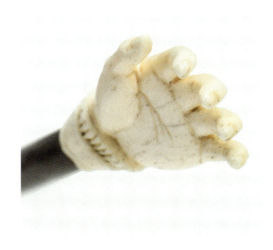

Backscratcher.
Inv. No. 7.815

Panel of textile samples: heavy silk ribbons. Inv. No. 61.682

Centre and Periphery

Vienna, a royal seat and capital city, was the undisputed centre of the Habsburg empire in the 19th century. Most of the goods purchased by its aristocratic and bourgeois classes of customer were not manufactured there, but at the edges of the empire. The two most important centres of decorative glass production were Murano near Venice and Gablonz in Bohemia. In terms of porcelain manufacture, Vienna and Bohemia were fierce competitors. Other centres in turn produced successful exports, such as scythes from the Eisenwurzen region or fezzes that were exported to the Orient. The manufacture of luxury items such as fine leather goods was concentrated in Vienna. Famous foreign prod-

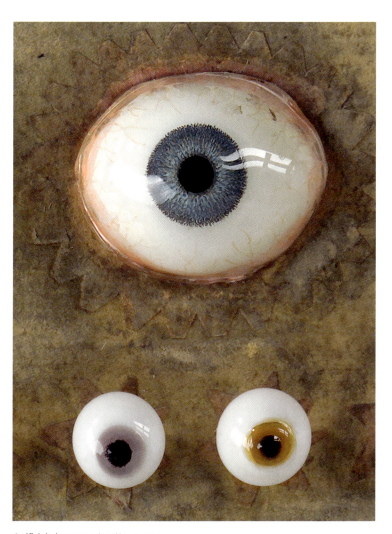

Artificial glass eyes. Inv. No. 30.134

ucts, such as English Wedgwood china, were copied for the domestic market.

The trade exhibitions that were held in the first half of the 19th century tended to be regional events. During its first and only World Exhibition in 1873, Vienna for a short time became the interface between East and West, the centre of the world even.

Agricultural Models

Scientists began to take an interest in agriculture in the 18th century. At home and abroad, models, among other things, spread awareness of new types of agricultural machine. In Vienna, Abbé Aloys Harder (1769-1857) built such models for the Agricultural Society that was founded in

1807 and for Kaiser Ferdinand's technological collection of over 1,000 models that covered the whole spectrum of agricultural tools and machines, ranging from ploughs and harrows to rakes and butter churns to machines for sowing, reaping, turning hay and threshing. Collections like this laid the foundations for agricultural engineering works.

Models of Machines

Luxury goods were the product of a high level of workmanship. The manufacture of mass-produced goods, on the other hand, went hand in hand with the introduction of machines. The Museum's collection of models allows visitors a glimpse of the early days of industrialization and work in factories. The selection here shows wood and metal-working machines as well as machines from the textile and paper-making industries. A waterwheel and a steam engine are two examples of prime movers. These models were made in the first half of the 19th century in the workshops of Vienna's Polytechnic Institute where they were used as aids in mechanical engineering classes but also as scale models for copies.

Model of a Jacquard loom, 1824. Inv. No. 12.508

In The Depot: 'Production Technology'

The 'k.k. National-Fabriksproduktenkabinett' (Imperial and Royal National Collection of Manufactured Goods) is the heart of the display on 'Manual and Industrial Production Technology' and provides an insight into a whole range of subjects: agriculture and forestry, wood and metal-working, textiles and clothing, food, beverages and tobacco, paper, glass and ceramics manufacture, as well as chemical production and plastics. In addition, there are other, extensive 19th and early 20th century collections of tools (Georg Altmütter's collection), locks and keys (Andreas Dillinger's collection), knives (Anton Petermandl's collection), models of agricultural implements (collection of the 'k.k. Niederösterreichische Landwirtschaftsgesellschaft', the Imperial and Royal Agricultural Society of Lower Austria) as well as an extensive collection of merchandise knowledge items. Among the Museum's other outstanding exhibits are the apparatus and furnishings for an alchemist's laboratory as well as a large number of 17th – 19th century apothecaries' jars (collection of Arthur Krupp, Wiener Hofapotheke).

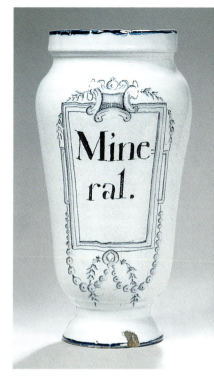

Apothecary's jar, c. 1800.
Inv. No. 11.322/195

A noteworthy exhibit in the display on 'Food, Beverages and Tobacco' is the model of the Vienna dairy around 1900 as made by the dairy workers themselves. This section also contains dioramas and models on the subject of tea, coffee, tobacco and chocolate processing. Austria's long history of textiles production is represented by a number of spinning wheels and mechanical spinning frames as well as by looms. The 'sewing hand' invented by the tailor Josef Madersperger is particularly significant: dating from the 1830s, it represents an important precursor of the sewing machine.
DuM

Everyday Life – Directions for Use

Everyday Life – Directions for Use

The Exhibition

We switch on a light in order to illuminate a space and give a feeling of safety to our surroundings. We measure humans and their movements, create categories for things around us, and organise spaces and cities. With vacuum cleaners we try to protect ourselves from dust; with locks against burglars. We dispose of garbage and, with a flush of the toilet, our 'human waste products' from view.

Many technical activities have become, in the course of time, natural behaviour patterns. We rarely ask what meaning all of these technologies has for us and our everyday life. Who thinks, for example, about our hygienic preconceptions when using a washing machine? We use technical equipment, and this in turn influences our expression, and our conceptions of how we arrange our life. Through their use, they define the way we live.

In this exhibition, these questions and the idea of 'naturalness' are reflected, 'technical behaviour patterns' and 'principles of technology' are sought out, and all are placed within the context of history and current debates.

At the centre of this exhibition lies the 'person/technology relationship'. The focus is on the meaning that the use of technical equipment has for humans. Central fields of investigation are the body, the house, the city and the environment. The time period covered is between the 1880s and the end of the 20th century.

A Tour: Themes of the Exhibition

Starting points: Museum, collections, technology of everyday life
The history of everyday life as told in folklore museums was enhanced when technical museums took up the topic starting in the 1970s. Objects were (re)considered under new criteria.

This exhibition can be accessed from three different starting points. They are all dedicated to the museums' tasks of collecting and documenting, which are typically practiced behind closed doors. Topics are the histories of the development and transmission of the museumified object.

At the two side entrances, a path is suggested by the depository. The objects on view there are related to each of the following topics.

The exhibits in the middle starting point, at the entrance to the gallery, refer to the central question of the exhibition: 'How and for what do I use technical equipment?' Visitors are invited, with the aid of previous knowledge and personal experience, to decode the meaning and function of the devices. This topic is one of the 'thought bubbles' arranged throughout the gallery. At the interactive station titled 'the life of things', visitors can hear statements from various people on consumer goods.

The activity level of humans is the starting point for the arrangement of this exhibition. The different sections are designated with functional words, which clarify human actions in connection with technology. The selected terms specify in each case a category for objects and technologies from a range of different applications.

One of the 'thought bubbles' of the exhibition

wishing / imagining

Ordinary desires for comfort, automation and security are the basis of many technical developments. However, technical systems also affect our conceptions – on our body image, on the organization of our daily routines and on our security needs.

Four 'thought bubbles' throughout the gallery show conceptions, desires and fears, which we have in connection with technology, and which are dealt with from different perspectives in the exhibition.

Perfect functioning
The desire to increase life span and 'perfect' by means of engineered organisms is discussed, using the human body as an example.

This conception is taken up in exhibition areas *surveying / sorting* and *replacing / adding,* which visitors can enter by passing through the sorting exhibition – a glass display with diagrams of human proportions.

Conjuring instead of working
The desire that hard or unpleasant work will take care of itself is an old one, and is reflected in many fairy tales and legends. This thought bubble is concerned with techniques witch facilitate our everyday lives through automazation and rationalization – and also as found in depiction of leprechauns and elves. This concept is dealt with in the exhibition areas *supplying / consuming* and *driving / moving.*

Assuredly secure
The topic of this bubble is the desire for security and control. Consideration of the close linkage between protection and security, through disciplinary action and the securing of spaces, is taken up in the section *safeguarding / suvervising* in the south concourse. Visitors enter this area through air locks, suggesting a feeling of access control.

The term progress is often regarded with scepticism, but it continues to seem inseparable from technology, and connected with the thought 'always higher, farther, faster…'. The projections play with the promises, which confront us daily: Terms such as 'self-cleaning, convenient, self-explanatory, error-free, energy-saving' appear and disappear again – desires burst…

surveying / sorting
This part of the exhibition analyses the construction of norms and standards. Historical and present technical systems of units and measurement are examined, which serve to systemize of knowledge, bodies, areas, movement and utensils.

On the basis of anthropological measurements from the last third of the 19th century, this presentation concentrates on rationalization debates of the 1920/30s and 1950/60s.

Anthropometry
Through technical measuring procedures, humans aspire to a precisely measured scientific ideal, the 'right' measurement that suggests objectification. However, concepts of normalization and standardisation of samples, which make possible on the one hand the predictability, democratization standardization and production of our functional environment, can on the other hand also promote individual and social exclusion.

This topic gives an overview of the systematic inventory of the human body in numbers and pictures, as well as of the dangers of psychological classification of the uncharted body: classical phrenology, anthro-

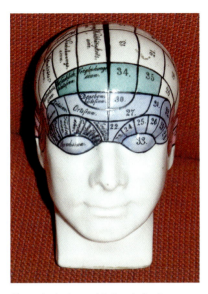

Phrenological porcelain head after Franz Joseph Gall (1758–1828). Inv. No. 58.896

pometry (criminal anthropology and anthropometric photography); National Socialist measurement practices; non-contact, automatic collection procedures of body characteristics in biometrics and measurement of 'sensory perception', such as hearing.

In this portion of the tour, the historical lines are further developed on the right, with interactive stations related to modern body measurement on the opposite side.

A light grid projection leads to the topics *lighting / highlighting* and *replacing / adding*. Readings of the exhibition visitor are sensitised, and each experienced moment is dissected immediately into time and volume units. Fragmenting the body into individual parts, which can be measured, made visible and replaced, forms the intersection of the two adjacent topics.

Measurement and rationalization of movement

Bodies, spaces and technology are placed in a systematic relationship to one another through measuring procedures. With the use of chronophotographic techniques, individual movements can be made visible, for example those of a swordsman or of a work routine. The rationalization of these motion sequences was first made first by spatial models, then through different screening tests, and today by means of CAD simulation. They permit ergonomic design and manufacturing of the work environment and of items we use in our daily lives. This can result in an adjustment of the machine to the body, and also to an adjustment of the body to the machine.

Everyday Life – Directions for Use

Tall cupboard from an original 'Frankfurter Küche', Margarete Schütte-Lihotzky. Bornheimer Hang Housing Development, Frankfurt, 1926–1930. Inv. No. 60.957

Rationalization of space

Measuring techniques and scientification have, particularly since the 1920s, intensified rationalization, and arranged the most diverse parts of everyday life in a comprehensive way.

The concept of the work kitchen and the associated representation of the scientification of housework serve as prominent examples of the rationalization of everyday life and its linkage with mechanization processes. The kitchen is the domestic space that will be examined first and foremost for its functional connections. Principles of scientific management introduced in the factory, workshop or in the office have been transferred to the household: The saving of time, energy, space, methods, and material play a role along with questions of ergonomics, mechanization and hygiene. As the most famous example, original furniture from a 'Frankfurter Küche' (Frankfurt Kitchen) designed by Margarete Schütte-Lihotzky is presented here as a rationalized kitchen adapted to a specific floor plan.

Urban planning and mass housing

These fields accompany modern urbanisation in a quantitative way (industrialization, growth of cities, population increase, social restructuring, supply, disciplinary action). The metropolis becomes the symbol of this rationalization process. Pre-fabricated building methods and the 'organisation of humans in adequate dwellings' are brought up for discussion in the context of the municipal buildings of Vienna, modern architecture as well as assembly plants.

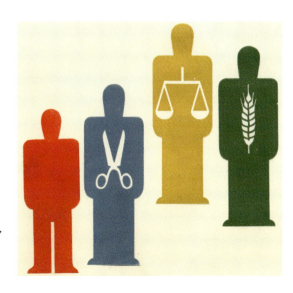

Pictograms of the 'Viennese method of picture statistics' developed by Otto Neurath (1882–1945)

Everyday Life – Directions for Use 105

Torso with leg prostetic. Demonstrations model, First World War. Inv. No. 33.933

replacing / adding

The history of technical replacement and extension with bodily prosthetics along with the idea of a changing body image are discussed in this part of the exhibition, on the basis the prosthesis collection of the Technisches Museum Wien from the time of the First World War, as well as modern prostheses. The idea of a 'normal, intact' body is analyzed. The design of the space includes an anatomical theatre. In its centre are two medical-anatomical teaching models, which show a comparison of the understanding of diverse parts of the body in the early 20th and 21st century.

Prosthetics

During the First World War, prosthesis technology experienced a great leap in development. Before 1914, arm prostheses served mainly to disguise the lack of a limb. The great demand of disabled veterans then provided an economic motivation for the development of functional prostheses. Additionally, a branch of cosmetic prostheses developed for so-called 'Sunday hands', allowing the user a return to 'normal' physical identity.

From the 1990s, computer-assisted prostheses like the C-Leg ('computerized leg', 1992) with integrated microelectronics recognised the prosthesis as more than a mere replacement. In an interactive station, at which visitors can

C-Leg. The first completely microprocessor-controlled leg prosthesis, 2004. Inv. No. 68.840

control the Myo Hand (sensor hand designed by Otto Bock) in a display case, one can see how the newest prosthesis technology functions, and which bodily functions are particularly supported.

Sensory prosthetics

A similar tendency can be seen in the case of sensory prosthetics: from the hearing aid to the invisible cochlea implant, from eyeglasses to the implanted photo-chip, physical sensors are developing with the support of micro-technology. Here again, the distinction between functional and decorative prosthesis can be seen.

Historical prostheses and the present state-of-the-art are shown on sample ears and eyes. A view through night-vision goggles demonstrates that 'prostheses' can also serve as an 'extension' of the body – equipment with abilities exceeding those naturally possessed by humans.

lighting / highlighting

Discussed here are aspects of the history of artificial lighting: Both the technical development of lights and their design in public and private spaces, and the history of light perception and appropriation. Along these lines, the visualisation, lighting and highlighting of the body is also treated.

Anatomical training model of a pregnant woman manufactured in 1680 by Stephan Zick, Nuernberg. Inv. No. 58.898

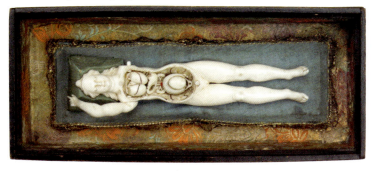

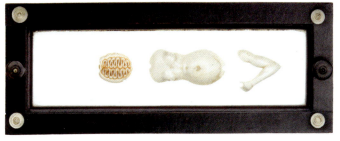

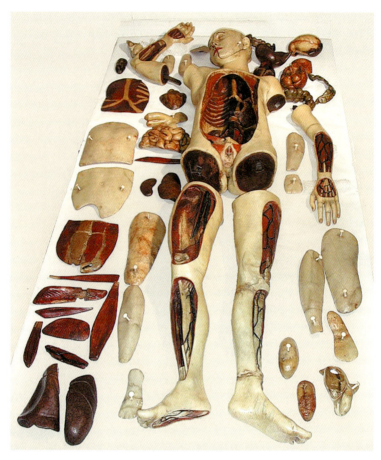

Life-size anatomical wax model from Hermann Praeuscher's Panopticon, ca. 1872. Inv. No. 60.653

highlighting – transparency of the body

Following *replacing /adding* is a tunnel, which shares space with a computer tomograph, illustrating the development of the highlighting of the human body.

The anatomical section, as a lightless forerunner, opened the inner body, and made representation of the spatial arrangement of individual parts possible.

With the development of endoscopy, doctors could use optical equipment to project light into a live human body, and later also during operating procedures. With new fibre optics as well as associated cold light systems, this technology can be used with decreasing risk.

The last tunnel segment is dedicated to picture-making procedures. The exhibit behind the tunnel draws a connection between viewing by means of technical equipment and the topic of psychoanalysis: The 'will to transparency' concerns even the un-lighted corners of the human psyche.

lightning – development of artificial light

Persistence and change characterize the development of the open flame to gaslight, electric bulb, fluorescent tubes and the modern LED (light emitting diode).

The technical facilities and developments are shown in six accessible displays. On one side the lights are shown, on the other, the related light is simulated, which gives an impression of the brightness, colour, and illumination of each. In the exhibition arrangement, chronology is subordinate to topical organisation, since nearly all developments in the history of artificial lighting continue to be used: Fluorescent tubes did not appear until the 1950s, but the open flame is still a popular lighting option.

As visitors enter the east concourse of the gallery, they come to a 'light shower', which suggests the topic through its brightness. Behind is found the area where the topics *lighting / highlighting* and *supplying / consuming* interconnect: euphoria for electricity and light. The spread of lighting systems and development of new phosphors was accompanied by a discourse over (artificial) light, which provoked, above all, overwhelming enthusiasm for electricity which was becoming bright, clean, and safe. The arc lamp was regarded as an artificial sun; electricity was allegorically represented and inspired visions. Its everyday use and acceptance was, however, a far cry from the initial enthusiasm.

Hanging gas 'Auer-light' with incandescent mantle, 1910. Inv. No. 17.236

The use of light in public spaces is represented in connection with urbanisation and the electrical grid that is necessary for street lighting. Also discussed is the use of light for the representation of political power as well as its use for recreational and personal consumption.

Starting in 1880 – and particularly into the 1920s – interior lighting became a substantial component of discourse in architecture, rationalization and hygiene. Lighting functions as a result of the interaction of illumination, lamp construction, lighting control, and interior and exterior building design. The appropriation of artificial lighting depends not only on technical possibilities, but also on pre-existing models of light perception and personal attitudes in relation to mechanization. With turn- and tilt-switches one can see how subtly the transition was designed for the use of a new form of energy: Thus, the early rotary switches for electric lights required the same hand movement as the potentiometer of the petroleum lamps that preceded them.

Light, self-presence and emotion are topics in the so-called 'light room'. Music as an acoustic element is combined with different lighting scenarios, which cause different moods.

Light bulb socket or electricity-drain. Sockets for light bulbs were used additionally as plug sockets, 1925. Inv. No. 60.637

supplying / consuming and transforming / preserving
Connecting to the section 'Energy' (2nd level), this area shows the development of networks and infrastructure as a pre-requisite for the supply of power generated with coal, gas and water. The transition from the urban to the domestic supply network – from the electricity-hog to the wall socket – also discussed are the question of the safety of the device and the application of new forms of energy. Also presented is the 'electrification of the body' in medical and domestic hygiene, in addition, as well as the danger of bodily injury the abuse of electrical devices presents. The intersection between the topics *safeguarding / supervising* (Hochquellwasserleitung/ spring-water main) and *disposing /concealing* (waste water network, drainage) forms the water supply network.

Warning illustration from 'Elektroschutz' ('Electrical Protection') by Stefan Jellinek, 1931

Sun-tanning light, 1920s. Inv. No. 24.480

Energy and 'vitality'
Energy flow through the body! This realization meant the development of a thermodynamic view of how the body works, replacing the purely mechanical one. The first systematic attempts to seize this energy took place with a focus on the human body.

Electro-therapy and electro-pathology
Along the wall is shown the effect electricity has had on humans in its electro-therapeutic (sun-tanning beds, electric massagers) and electro-pathological applications. From the collection of the former 'Elektropathologisches Museum' (electro-pathological museum), a set of wax bolus, diagrams and information to on the diagnosis of disease attest to the explosive effect of the topic.

Power supply – energy consumption
The nets are crossed 'physically': lines for gas, electricity and water criss-cross laterally, above and below the installation. A map shows the development of the supply networks for Vienna and Lower Austria.

The mass-electrification of the household was made possible by the coexistence of gas and electricity, and shaped by marketing strategies,

Electric toaster 'OMEGA', 1930s. Inv. No. 31.089

Everyday Life – Directions for Use

'The housewife goes out…', ca. 1920

safety questions, the distribution of equipment and knowledge level of the population. The electric plug – the so-called electricity-hog – stands in opposition to the electric meter. Small gas and electrical devices show the variety of cooking devices as well as their multi-functionality – for example with so-called 'Volksgriller' (personal griller) – and documents the fashion of exotic ways of cooking. Three groups of equipment demonstrate how our handling of energy has changed: The stove, the furnace, and the refrigerator. The latter draws a connection with the following topic.

transforming / preserving

For this topic, a comparison is made between the preparation and preservation of food and the production of building materials. In a building material factory bricks, terrazzo and concrete are manufactured just like meringues, currant cake and semolina pudding; in all cases chemical-physical reactions take place, such as a transformation by heat. The building material examples appear in the section on mass housing *(surveying / sorting)*.

In the pantry, the conservation and preservation of food is discussed in the context of preservation jars, bottles and crockery. Different exhibits show the development of iceboxes and coolers.

driving / moving

A round showcase and a turntable – connected by a drive-shaft – command the area. Some devices can be set in motion with a crank on the side, while others are activated with the push of a button.

With the shifting of action and effort from the body to the equipment, the specific body movements of human interaction – e.g. the push of a button, or a step of the foot – have been reduced over time until the near 'retirement' of the body with a sensor switch. This process is demonstrated on the basis the development of the electrical fractional horsepower motor as well as different groups of equipment: Household and do-it-yourself enthusiast devices, sewing machines, razors, wash devices, and multi-functional devices. As motors are becoming ever smaller, it is also evident that many devices will continue to become lighter, more mobile and wireless.

Cutting, Grating, Boring, Stirring...

The groups of household and do-it-yourself enthusiast devices are each assigned to an activity. Steps in automation are shown from the bottom upward, e.g. from the gimlet to the drill press; from the fork, to the whisk, to the mixer. All devices were dependent on the physical employment of the body turning a crank – which was then automated using gears – until the flow of energy could activated with the push of a button.

Washing

The increasing automation of the lengthy and hard work of laundry is shown through the development of different washing devices up to the fully automatic washing machine. From a technical perspective, the washing machine utilizes three engines, which propel clothes in different movements.

Sewing

The sewing machine represents, from a mechanical perspective, a completely self-contained piece of equipment. The electric motor is now used instead of the human foot, otherwise the equipment has remained essentially unchanged. It became particularly important for the housework of women. In this connection, child sewing machines with guidance booklets for the doll mother attests to the socialization of girls.

Shaving

The series of saving razors shows that the introduction of the electric motor involved not only a change in hand movement, but also new developments in cutting and blade technology.

Sucking, Ventilating, Blowing
A showcase is dedicated to those devices, which could only be developed with the use of the electrical fractional horsepower motor: Hair dryer, vacuum cleaner and fan.

All-in-one
Opposite of the genesis of the electrical fractional horsepower motor is a set of multi-functional devices showing the universal applicability of the engine mount, to which various devices can be attached.

Rulin, bottle for insect control, ca. 1950. Inv. No. 36.368

safeguarding / supervising
Drawing on three parts of the collection, the emergence of techniques and mechanisms for protection are shown: the development of hygiene – safeguarding from dirt, dust and illness, and security technology – protection from other humans and the fire-brigade.

Safeguarding procedures frequently fall back on standard conceptions of purity, illness and property. These procedures make possible the introduction of practices of securing and exclusion that increase the potential for surveillance and disciplinary action.

Development of hygiene
An exceptional discourse on hygiene began at the end of the 19th century, focusing on protection techniques against dirt and dust. Along with industrialization and urbanisation, the concept of hygiene became a comprehensive 'everyday life science', and an approach to varied municipal and political policies.

Techniques of scientific perception, technical (device) developments and patterns of social thought are not related to the topic of hygiene in a direct or linear way, but rather have a mutual effect on each other.

On the basis of this question, from when something is categorized as dust and connected with illness, the scientific methods of dust and disease research are discussed, as is the popularization of these discoveries. Also taken up are techniques of fighting against dirt and illness in the varied contexts of bodily, industrial, household and city hygiene. The public arena and industry are brought up for discussion – street development as well as early measures to protect workers at their jobs, which was motivated in a large part by health damage attributed to

Electric vacuum cleaner, 'BONZO', 1930s. Inv. No. 30.356

dust. In the 'hygienic home' are, on the one hand, the familiar devices for dust suppression, and on the other, publicised materials such as linoleum, which guarantees a clean floor surface. Laundry care is discussed in the context of detergents and washing devices as well as irons and techniques for pest control. In the area of personal hygiene, in both public swimming pools and the private bath, habits are influenced by rising hygiene standards. Here, the technical development of hygiene and hygiene products is shown. In the direction of *supplying / consuming* visitors will find the topic of clean water and its supply to the city. Based on historical models for well-digging, as well as the famous Wiener Hochquellwasserleitung (Vienna spring-water main) is this section addresses aspects of water supply using the example of Vienna.

Securing
The lock and key collection refers to a further aspect of safeguarding and. In the so-called 'safe room', a cubic space in the gallery, different kinds of locks are presented from the latch plate up to modern securing systems, which have the ability to expand, and at the same time monitor, the secured area. In addition is shown, the types of things which have been secured over time, and how security needs and estimates of secured articles has changed.

Fire-brigade
The historical fire-brigade collection is thematically related to that of municipal service equipment. A selection of fire-fighting vehicles from

the late 19th and early 20th century, as well as a large number of fire-extinguishing devices, show how fire hazards are handled and fought.

disposing / concealing

Waste management cuts up, converts, swallows, passes on, separates and above all produces much that is not in our view. By observing the technical handling of wastewater, solid waste and human waste at public and private 'toilets', one can see that the meaning and function of this technology has changed very much. Conceptions of hygiene as well as shame borders and requirements of orderliness- and recently economic factors- increasingly affect the handling of human waste, rubbish and wastewater.

Toilets

At the intersection of *supplying / consuming* and *safeguarding / supervising*, the history of public facilities is told with an original *pissoirs* from 1900. Behind it, in six 'toilet rooms', the technical development of the domestic water closet is explained – from the chamber pot, the bourgeois velvet stool and the 'plunger closet' to flush toilets, up to the 'high-tech toilet.' The shame-ridden and hygienically motivated removal of human waste and odour is discussed at the same time. Beneath an exposed street, one can enter this zone of 'concealment'.

Public restroom on Sachsenplatz, Vienna, before its transfer to the museum.
Inv. No. 60.977

Waste Water
The topic of 'waste water disposal' follows directly from the water supply network and history the Wiener Hochquellwasserleitung. The many diverse techniques of waste water disposal are mentioned, from the covering and canalization of streams, which became the first waste water gutters, up to the 'Cholera Kanal' and the construction of the famous Viennese canal system, as well as a discussion of how the canals are maintained. The large wall illustration of a street gully, which filters rough material out of the wastewater, leads into the schematic representation of a purification plant.

Solid Waste
The many diverse strategies of rubbish disposal with the help of technical equipment are presented on the opposite wall: Repairing, separation and collection, re-evaluation, recycling and single-use disposable. Also dealt with are the rising quantity of rubbish, the increasingly diverse composition of waste and the well-known disposal strategies of recycling, land filling and waste incineration.

   The complexity of these facilities is explained as well, along with the composition of the processed material and that of the final 'remainder' – which must, even after a long time, be concealed and maintained in a secure repository.
NoL

medien.welten

The exhibition entitled 'medien.welten' considers the emergence of the media in the modern age: from postal routes, telegraph and telephone cables to radio and television stations and the Internet, a worldwide network has developed over time for the transmission of news. At the same time, technologies have been developed to capture the fleeting moment: the advent of printing allowed thoughts to be recorded on paper; photography and film record visual impressions; the phonograph and the gramophone conserve sound. Calculators, typewriters, punched card machines and computers have been used to store and process large amounts of data. Since it has had access to the immense wealth of texts, data, images and sounds on the Internet, the now ubiquitous PC has blurred the boundaries between means of storage and means of transmission.

In the centrally located gallery, groups of iconic exhibits take visitors on a short tour of the history of the media, and data terminals give summary information on all the topics considered in the exhibition. Historical exhibits, together with illustrations and descriptions, are located in the surrounding aisles. Fundamental principles – such as counting on an abacus – are illustrated by means of mechanical and electronic 'hands-on' installations. Additional data terminals permit further reading on the history of the media, divided into ten topics and thirteen eras. Logged on with their personal 'smart.card', visitors can select which language they view texts in. Moreover, the 'smart.card' allows visitors to collect digital content in their own virtual 'rucksack'. Using their card number, they have on-line access to that content after their visit.

The latest media are also on display in the exhibition. A stereoscopic projection encourages visitors to participate in rather an unusual chess game in which their opponent is a projected fairground figure in historical Turkish costume. The chessboard, too, is merely a projection.

Visitors can immerse themselves in the world of virtual reality in the Museum's virtual reality theatre. A panorama format on the curved screen and a stereophonic sound system create a virtual world in three dimensions. Using laser rods, each member of the audience can intervene in the action.

Letterboxes

Transmission media

Of Messengers, Riders and Stagecoaches: the Postal Service

A modern postal service developed in Europe after 1500. Staging posts where riders and horses were changed were set up at regular intervals along principal routes. Riders carried letters in large leather bags. The first relay postal services carried only royal mail, but soon accepted business correspondence for a fee. Making use of the news that arrived regularly with the post, 17th century newspapers began to be published on post days.

Vienna's first private city post office opened in 1772. Its postmen carried tin boxes in which they collected letters and noisily announced their arrival by shaking clappers with metal fittings. The growing amount of private, business and government correspondence led to the introduction of letterboxes, stamps and envelopes. Postmarks indicated the route and time taken by letters. Besides letters and parcels, public stagecoaches also carried travellers at scheduled times for a fixed fee. Where post routes crossed, the times of connecting services were agreed. It became possible to calculate travelling time; printed distance tables, route maps and travel guides meant routes could be planned. Printed rules regulated travel and stood for state control.

Telegraphy

Around 1800 in France, Claude Chappe built a visual signal line of his own design. Each of its stations had a mast with a crossbeam to whose

Telegraphy apparatus

ends pairs of movable arms were attached. A telegraphist positioned the arms; another telegraphist at the next station read the positions by means of a telescope and relayed the signal down the line until it reached its destination. The meaning of the positions assumed by the arms was secret and unknown even to the telegraphists. Such visual telegraphs were for the sole use of the state.

The electric telegraph became established after 1845, initially on the railways. It quickly developed into an independent system for the dissemination of news. In the case of the system devised by the American Samuel F. B. Morse, a telegraph key was tapped to produce combinations of long and short sound signals representing numbers and letters. At the receiving end, the signals were recorded as dots and dashes on a paper strip. David E. Hughes later developed a telegraph instrument that was easier to use in that telegrams were typed in and printed out in plain text.

The increasing importance of telegraphy led to mergers between national telegraph networks and the formation of an international network with standardized operating systems and tariffs. Exchanges employing hundreds of female telegraphists formed the hub of the network that served government agencies but mainly trade and industry. News agencies like Reuters in London gathered news from around the world by electric telegraph and sold it to newspapers and businesses.

Going Underground: Pneumatic Dispatch

For the transmission of urgent news within the city, Vienna in 1875 developed an underground pneumatic dispatch system that – away from the increasing volume of traffic – directly connected post offices and telegraph exchanges. Metal canisters containing letters and telegrams were conveyed through the system by compression or exhaustion of air. Items were removed, sorted and forwarded at intermediate points. Hundreds of red letterboxes and dozens of dispatching stations in post offices and telegraph offices were available for users of the pneumatic letter service.

Pneumatic dispatch system. Inv. No. 54.630

The Telephone

On the basis of the telephone patent granted to him in 1876, the Scottish-born American Alexander G. Bell founded a successful private telephone company in the United States. In Austria, companies began to operate local telephone networks in some cities during the 1880s. They were taken into state ownership at the end of the 19th century when the Austrian Post Office began to build inter-city telephone lines, exchanges and public telephone booths.

To make a call, a magneto was cranked up to call the telephone exchange. The (lady) operator answered the call and connected the caller by inserting the two ends of a cord in the relevant sockets on her switchboard. As manual exchanges were soon unable to cope with the growth in calls, systems were automated after 1910 using a principle devised by Almon G. Strowger. The caller connected himself to the number he wanted by dialling the rotary dial on his telephone. In the telephone exchange, a metal pin called the brush moved to the terminal that corresponded to the dialled number.

Telephony became problematic over long distances because of the weakening signal. Viennese Robert von Lieben developed an electronic tube that amplified signals. Telephone conversations up to a distance of 1,000 kilometres now became possible.

medien.welten

'Adcock' radio direction finder. Inv. No. 56.266

Wireless Communication: Radio

In the 1910s in Great Britain, Guglielmo Marconi's company built land stations that used radio waves to communicate with merchant ships and warships at sea. Initially, Morse signals were used, but improved radio transmitters were able to produce high frequencies capable of transmitting sound. Before World War I, the German company Telefunken equipped the German and Austro-Hungarian armies with radio sets – from those for use on board warships to portable sets for use in the field. Transmissions were encoded to prevent the enemy from listening in.

Telecommunications were essential to the Third Reich's preparations for World War II. Before war began, the civilian telegraph and telephone systems as well as the Luftwaffe's wire communications system and radio network were improved to meet military requirements. When war started, the networks were extended to the front. Every fifth member of the German armed forces worked in communications. Hitler waged his war of conquest on this basis from bunkers behind the lines. The German military command directed its troops, tanks, aircraft and U-boats through radio communications that were encoded using the 'Enigma' coding machine. Devices such as the American 'Adcock' radio direction finder, on the other hand, made it possible to locate the enemy through his radio signals.

A 'Wire to the World': Radio

Commercial broadcasting began in the United States in the early 1920s. In Vienna, RAVAG was Austria's state-run 'wire to the world' after 1924. It broadcast music and official news. To begin with, the broadcasting industry manufactured simple crystal sets with long wire antennas; headphones were needed to hear the weak signal. More costly devices were devised with amplifiers and loudspeakers that were able to fill a room with sound. An attachment called a 'radioscope' was available in Vienna; it was a projector for film strips made of paper that illustrated certain RAVAG radio broadcasts.

In the Third Reich, the Ministry of Propaganda in Berlin was in charge of radio programmes. Manufacturers had to produce a cheap and standardized 'Volksempfänger' (People's Receiver) that every 'national com-

*US437 Ingelen Geographic wireless set.
Inv. No. 55.108*

rade' could afford. All of Germany was to hear Hitler's inflammatory speeches – except Jews, who were forbidden from owning radio sets. In 1938, the still cheaper 'Deutscher Kleinempfänger' (Small German Receiver) was launched. Foreign radio stations could not be heard on it; it received signals only from the nearest Reich transmitter. When war started in 1939, listening to 'enemy radio stations' became punishable by death. The new law was to ensure that the Nazi regime's radio propaganda could not be refuted by outside sources such as the BBC.

A 'Window on the World': Television

Electronic television is mainly based on the iconoscope camera tube that Vladimir K. Zworykin developed in the 1920s and 30s when working in the United States. Its electron beam scans an image line-by-line. Depending on the brightness of any given point on the image, the cur-

*Schönbrunn Studio made television in Austria possible after the 1950s.
Inv. No. 54.445*

rent of the electron beam is modified. Different electrical impulses reassemble the image on the screen of a receiving tube. In standard television broadcasting, the picture is then broadcast via transmitters to viewers' receivers.

The mass production of television sets began after the war in the United States, making them affordable for vast numbers of people. In Austria, post office and radio engineers experimented with the medium. Once television sets went into production, television broadcasts could begin. From August 1955, the Österreichischer Rundfunk broadcast a short and improvised programme three times a week from a tiny studio. Starting in January 1957, there was about 20 hours of programming a week, broadcast daily except Tuesdays. In the early days, people went to inns or visited their neighbours if they wanted to watch television, but it quickly became the done thing to have a television set of one's own. The television became the focus of attention in the home, as much a status symbol as a 'window on the world'.

Wooden manual printing press.
Inv. No. 14.029

Storage media

Writings for the People: Woodblock and Letterpress Printing

In the 15th century, woodblock printing spread throughout Europe as a means of reproducing images of saints, prayers, playing cards or calendar leafs. A mirror image composition was cut into a woodblock. When finished, the design could not be changed. It was then inked and pressed onto paper. In contrast, around 1450 Johannes Gutenberg began to cast individual metal letters that were composed into lines and pages within an adjustable hand-mould. When the printing process was completed, the letters could be taken apart again. Printed matter was

'Brunsviga' calculating machine. Inv. No. 29.423

soon in wide circulation and promoted literacy. Starting in the 16th century, reformers such as Martin Luther used pamphlets to question and attack papal authority. The spiritual and secular authorities reacted by censoring him.

Between 1751 and 1780, Denis Diderot and Jean d'Alembert published the multi-volume *Encyclopédie* in Paris. In the spirit of the Enlightenment, it collected the knowledge of its day and illustrated it copiously using copperplate engravings. Occasionally banned by the censors, it nonetheless circulated widely throughout Europe.

In Munich around 1800, Alois Senefelder developed an inexpensive printing process called lithography that enabled him to reproduce short texts or music quickly and in limited numbers. Using a greasy crayon, he drew a design on a smooth piece of limestone. Once fixed, it was wetted and rolled with oily ink that adhered only to the greasy drawing (being damp, the rest of the surface repelled the ink). After that a print could be taken. Lithographic printing offices sprung up immediately in numerous European centres where maps, posters, pamphlets, portraits and landscapes were produced.

Arithmetic with Gears

The growth in administration by the state and commercial underwriters lead to an increase in the computational load. In use since ancient times, the handy abacus was replaced by calculating machines that made use of cogs and gears. A handle was turned to perform addition; it was reversed to perform subtraction; multiplication was performed through repeated addition, while division was performed through repeated subtraction. Around 1820, the director of two insurance companies in Paris, Charles Xavier Thomas, patented a calculating machine for the four arithmetical operations. It worked on the principle of the mechanical calculator constructed by Gottfried Wilhelm Leibniz in the 17th century.

In the 19th century, the British mathematician Charles Babbage compiled the first reliable actuarial tables. He also worked on astronomical tables for navigation purposes. With the financial backing of the British government, he began constructing a Difference Engine for the compu-

Le Taxiphote: a stereoscopic viewer.
Inv. No. 16.728

tation of numerical sequences. Babbage's attempt failed, however, because of the imprecision of the gears available to him. In 1833, he conceived the Analytical Engine, a programmable calculating machine whose structure was very similar to today's computers, even if it was composed solely of mechanical parts.

Pictures for your Enjoyment

For centuries, pictures were a rarity. In the 19th century, however, a colourful and essentially bourgeois pictorial culture developed. Rotundas contained monumental and realistic panoramas of cities or historic events. Camera obscuras were built at vantage points. Images of the surrounding view were projected by a rotating angled mirror in the roof onto a horizontal surface inside for viewers to gaze at in wonder. With the Magic Lantern, images painted on glass plates were projected onto the wall of a darkened room. Later design innovations allowed images to move and dissolve. There were even special effects like artificial fog for those *really scary* pictures!

Changing illumination of scenic paintings called dioramas simulated changes in the time of day. The English physicist Charles Wheatstone invented the 'stereoscope', a device that takes two photographs of the same object from slightly different angles based on the distance between the eyes. When viewed together, the photographs give an impression of depth and solidity. In his 'magical optical discs', the Austrian Simon Stampfer exploited the physical phenomenon of 'persistence of vision'. It means that still pictures when shown in rapid succession give the impression of movement. Like various other optical toys, so-called 'zoetropes' were popular forms of entertainment in the homes of the bourgeoisie.

Capturing the Fleeting Moment: Photography

In 1839, the French scene painter Louis J. M. Daguerre succeeded in fixing a photographic picture by exposing an iodized silver plate to light and developing the image in fumes of mercury. In Vienna, the mathematician Josef Petzval, in collaboration with the optician Friedrich Voigtländer, made important advances in the construction of lenses: exposure times were greatly reduced and portrait photography flourished as a result. Draped in front of backcloths and held immobile in

Photographic reproduction

special chairs, the wealthy classes in particular had their photographs taken in countless studios. Recruits and criminals had their photographs taken for army and police records. Explorers and travellers documented foreign lands and peoples. The wet collodion process that was used required plates to be prepared before exposure and developed immediately in a portable darkroom, however. The dry plate and handier cameras simplified photography and allowed growing numbers of tourists to take their own photographs. The introduction of celluloid film gave yet more impetus to amateur photography. By 1900, processes had been developed for the mass printing of photographs. Georg Meisenbach invented the half-tone process in which the photographic surface is exposed through an optical screen. The image is broken up into dots that are heavier in dark areas of the image and lighter in brighter areas. All shades of grey can be reproduced in this way and printed in rotary presses.

medien.welten

The steam-powered printing press brings about the popular press

Printing Presses, Typesetting Machines and The Popular Press
Newspaper printing was first industrialised in England. Newspaper circulation rose, the cost of newspapers fell and the popular press came about. The Leipzig printer Friedrich König developed a steam-powered printing press in which a cylinder moved over the flatbed bearing the sheet of paper, pressing it against the type forme. The follow-up model, with two impression cylinders, went into service at the *Times* of London in 1814. In Philadelphia between 1863 and 1865, William A. Bullock built a rotary press in which the type forme was attached to a rotating cylinder; an impression cylinder provided the pressure. Bullock's press had two type formes and impression cylinders to permit printing on both sides in one operation. Sheets of paper still had to be cut and inserted manually into the press, however. John Walter III, the proprietor of the London *Times*, had a rotary press built that printed on a continuous roll of paper taken from a reel. After printing, the newspaper sheets, printed on both sides, were cut at a rate of 12,000 per hour. Beginning in 1872, Vienna's *Neue Freie Presse* was the first newspaper in mainland Europe to be printed on a continuous roll of paper using rotary presses. Its circulation rose from 10,000 copies in the year it was founded – 1864 – to 35,000 in 1873.

In the 1880s, the German-born American Ottmar Mergenthaler automated the process of typesetting with his Linotype. Working at a keyboard, a compositor selected the letter moulds he needed; complete lines of type were then cast from them and assembled into pages. Mergenthaler's Linotype ('line o' type') enabled a single compositor to set thousands of letters an hour. It turned its inventor into a successful businessman – and more than a few compositors out of a job.

Typewriter by Peter Mitterhofer.
Inv. No. 14.070

Writing, Filing, Counting: the Office

The administration required by trade and industry gave rise to the modern office. Numerous designers, including Peter Mitterhofer from South Tyrol, developed writing machines with which texts could be written quickly in a clear typeface. In 1874, the firm of Remington & Sons began manufacture of the typewriter developed by Sholes and Glidden in the United States. The shift key for capitalization, four rows of keys and their positions as well as touch-typing subsequently became standard. The Underwood 1 model made by the Wagner Typewriter Co. in 1895 for the first time allowed the typist a direct view of the sheet being typed. Phonographs like the 'dictaphon' were used to record dictations. Files allowed the systematic storage of documents. Office work was usually done by women.

The populace, too, was administered by machine. Reducing individuals to characteristics like gender and age, regular censuses had been carried out since the 18th century to allow planning of tax revenue and recruitment needs. For the 1890 census in the United States, Hermann Hollerith developed a punched card system for the analysis of millions of forms. Punched holes in cards indicated particular characteristics. A machine was able to recognise the position of the holes and file the cards accordingly. Hollerith's technique was adopted in Austria that same year.

Engraved in Wax – Phonography

In 1878, Thomas Alva Edison succeeded in making a mechanical recording of sound. The phonograph is based on his observation that sound waves cause a diaphragm to vibrate. With a vibrating stylus, he made impressions on a sheet of tinfoil attached to a rotating cylinder. By drawing the stylus back along the sound track, he was able to reproduce the recorded sound. The use of wax cylinders greatly improved sound reproduction. In 1888, Edison was finally able to market the phonograph which could easily be used to make sound recordings for

Berlin Standard Gramophone and 'Nipper'. Inv. Nos. 35.246, 35.247

personal or business use. The mass production of wax cylinders for commercial purposes was costly because each cylinder had to be recorded individually. For singers with powerful voices, recordable wax cylinders meant the beginning of a new career.

To circumvent Edison's patents, Emil Berliner experimented with wax-coated zinc disks. When a speaker spoke into the horn, a stylus cut through the wax coating and cut a groove in the bare metal underneath. From this, a matrix of the disk was then produced using which large numbers of copies were pressed onto celluloid or shellac.

'Living Pictures': the Movies

Like other photographers of the day, the German Ottomar Anschütz also experimented with sequential pictures. His electrical, coin-operated 'Schnellseher' (quick viewer) used rotating discs to show still images blending into continuous movement. Thomas A. Edison developed the kinetoscope, a coin-operated peep show that ran a 15-metre-long celluloid film for the viewer. The Lumière brothers presented their Cinématographe to the public in Paris in 1895. It used sprocket-wound film and was both a camera and a projector. In 1896, 'living' pictures were

Living pictures

also shown in Vienna. Only a short while later, the cinema became a metropolitan institution. The film market in Europe and America flourished even before World War I. Films were still silent then and were usually shown with live musical accompaniment. Lengthy experiments were required before synchronous speech could be reproduced successfully. *The Jazz Singer* starring Al Jolson was the first talking motion picture in 1927. Hollywood began to produce 'talkies'. They often had fairy-tale qualities that allowed their viewers a brief escape from harsh lives. In both world wars, virulent propaganda films and weekly newsreels stirred up hate for the enemy.

The 'Cinématographe' by the Lumière Brothers. Inv. No. 13.294

Electronic Data Processing

Whether maintaining supplies, running the Reich Labour Service, keeping men in active service or even organising the deportation and murder of the Jews, the Third Reich's war machinery functioned largely using punched card technology. Powerful computers performed aeronautical and ballistic calculations. At Bletchley Park north of London, the British built the 'Colossus' computer to help decipher the codes of the German 'Enigma' encoding machine. After the war, computers such

The transistor-based 'Mailüfterl' computer. Inv. No. 19.110

medien.welten 133

'Chess-playing Turk' – an installation

as the American 'UNIVAC' were operated in commercial computer centres that sold computing time to clients. Such computers contained a large number of highly sensitive electronic tubes. If a single tube failed during an arithmetic process, the whole process had to be repeated. The advent of the transistor marked a significant improvement, however: it was more reliable, smaller and above all cheaper. In Austria in 1958, Heinz Zemanek built the 'Mailüfterl' computer, a transistor-based computer for research purposes. The development by American engineers of the silicon chip – a tiny wafer of semi-conducting material that can contain thousands of transistors – ushered in the age of microelectronics. Computers became smaller and more powerful. Used to control production, they initiated an unprecedented wave of automation in industry. Teleprocessing caught on in offices in the 1960s. Workplaces with only a keyboard and a screen are now linked by cable to a remote central computer where data are processed. In many head offices, such systems are used for accounting, stock control and the payment of wages. Data protection guidelines have been established to avoid the invasion of privacy.

BRAVE NEW MEDIA WORLD

In the post-war period, radios and televisions, telephones and cameras, video and sound recorders became the consumer goods of the media industry with increasing numbers of people able to afford them. Transistor radios and car phones meet the demand for greater mobility.

Answering machines record phone calls when no one is home. Cellular radio systems have turned the conventional phone into the mobile phone; those who own one can be reached anywhere at any time. Electronic calculators and typewriters found their way into offices. Whole letters can be faxed through phone lines. The home PC was initially used mainly for simple computer games but is now being used to manage the annual budget and do word-processing. As functionality improves, it is becoming the media machine for everyone. In the 1990s, improved processing power allowed sophisticated sound and picture editing. Via the Internet, programmes and multi-media content can be downloaded from anywhere and redirected anywhere. Now with links to cellular radio systems, mobile phones can be used to surf the Net even when one is out and about. This brave new media world ensures that users of the Internet have the whole world within their reach. They are promised it all, now – albeit only in the form of a digital image. What is more, every step taken in this digital world leaves tracks that can be followed. Those who venture into this brave new media world run the risk of having their activities monitored and their secrets aired by today's information technologies.
MoO, PeW

The digital revolution – Personal Computer and Internet

Musical Instruments

Musical Instruments

Instruments from different times: Renaissance portative and Baroque positive. Inv. Nos. 15.296 and 15.288

THE ORIGINS OF THE COLLECTION OF MUSICAL INSTRUMENTS IN THE TECHNISCHES MUSEUM WIEN

The collection of musical instruments is a root of the Museum and is largely derived from the two institutions out of which the Museum has evolved, the 'Technologisches Gewerbemuseum' and the 'Museum der Geschichte der Österreichischen Arbeit'. As instrument making flourished in Vienna especially in the 19th century, the craft was an obvious choice for inclusion in the planned Technisches Museum. Moreover, numerous self-playing automatons and mechanical instruments lend the collection a special, technological quality.

The Concept in Brief

Many things influence a musical instrument: inventiveness, craftsmanship, experimentation, tradition, aesthetics and different tonal qualities. How is an instrument made? What does it sound like? What kind of relationship does it develop with a composer and a performer? Which instruments play automatically? These questions and more are answered using groups of instruments. Mechanical musical instruments and technical solutions that record and reproduce previously 'ephemeral' events greatly extend the range of conventional instruments. The system of trial and error that has given rise to today's new instruments is described as is the software used in music typography and other recording media.

Visitors enter the exhibition through staged piano and organ 'workshop' areas that describe the instruments, their development, makers, uses and functions. Models illustrate the development of the hammer action and the function of the organ trackers. Towards the centre of the room, self-playing variations on the piano and organ are assembled around the topic 'automatons'. In a small 'cinema', visitors can retrieve film and sound samples of the most important instruments. Six 'wired-for-sound' armchairs invite visitors to access audio clips on demand to learn about the associated field of piano and organ.

Media stations give details about instrument making today and lecterns are equipped with index cards containing yet more details. A number of instruments can be demonstrated during guided tours.

The Organ

The organ is a complex musical instrument with many mechanical, electric and pneumatic parts that work together to vibrate the air in its pipes so as to produce sounds. Like no other instruments, organs produce completely different sound patterns depending on where and when they were built. In antiquity, the organ was used during circus performances and gladiatorial contests; it was later played for entertainment at court and has had a home in Christian churches for around 1,200 years. The organ, like no other instrument, has over time undergone major modifications as dictated by prevailing tastes, up to imitating orchestras and today's historicized replicas.

With self-playing devices and effect stops in salon and cinema instruments, the organ returned to the secular sphere in the 20th century, most especially at fairgrounds.

The Organ Builder's Workshop

In terms of size, tonal design and body, each individual organ must be adapted to suit its intended purpose and the space it will occupy. This is why organs are still manufactured in workshops where craftsmen must be trained in a wide range of skills that enables them to use different materials and manufacturing methods. Some organ makers specialize in the manufacture of pipes or mechanical parts and thus act as sub-contractors. Large workshops manufacture everything themselves.

Current production methods are explained at a media station.

A founding furnace and casting bench are used to make the metal plate for organ pipes. Different types of wind chest, organ components and their respective tools are also on display. A chest of drawers shows the stages involved in creating different pipe forms. 'Organ Restoration' considers a topic that is important for a museum.

The Organ – A Distinctive Instrument

Different shapes and sizes of organ are built according to how the instrument is to be used. Besides static church organs with several keyboards for the hands (the 'manual') and a keyboard for the feet (the 'pedal'), there are small organs for use in chapels, schools and small

Organ builder's workshop

halls as well as for music making in the home. They usually have only one manual and no pedal, and their very names indicate that they can be readily carried: portative and positive, derived from the Latin 'portare' (to carry) and 'ponere' (to put).

Compact ceremonial organs were carried on processions of secular and religious dignitaries. Small instruments containing only pipes with reed work are called 'regals'.

On display are four instruments that symbolize the varied development of the organ: a portable processional organ (c. 1590), a reconstruction of an 'apfelregal' by Hans Weiditz (c. 1518), a baroque positive from the first half of the 18th century and, from the chapel at the Hofburg, the organ played by Anton Bruckner for many years. Three models of actions show in detail how the connections between keys and pipes function.

Reed instruments

Originally in organ pipes, an air column was made to vibrate. By the 15th century at the latest, however, organ pipes existed in which sounds were produced by small, vibrating metal plates ('tongues'). When air is forced through the pipes, the tongues strike a metal groove, which results in a rattling sound that can be modified using horns to produce a sound ranging from bellowing out to trumpet-like, or one that imitates the human voice ('vox humana' stop).

Following a change in musical tastes, organ builders in the 18th century tried to influence the volume of the organ's sound. This led to the adoption of free-reeds that had long been known outside of Europe. They vibrate freely in a slit, and their volume is modified by variations in air pressure.

Based on this principle, numerous types of instrument were made whose development was pioneered in Vienna at the beginning of the 19th century; among them are the 'physharmonica', the harmonium, the accordion and the mouth organ.

Examples of each type are on display.

Self-playing organs

The first automatic organs in the 16th century contained a cylinder whose pins were traced by a finger-like mechanism. By the 17th century, they had a wide tonal range and several ranks. Spring-driven or weight-operated, they were mounted in clocks, cupboards and other items of furniture and were known as flute clocks.

The 19th century was the heyday of the barrel organ, both large and small. Some barrel organs even had their own percussion instruments and flowery decoration – the orchestrion, for instance. They can still occasionally be heard at fairgrounds or in pedestrian precincts in cities during the summer.

At the turn of last century, the use of compressed air and perforated strips of paper or cardboard found favour as a controlling mechanism. This method allowed music of almost any length to be played. Four examples of such automatic instruments are on display: barrel organs in a cabinet and a Biedermeier writing bureau incorporating organ works, a small orchestrion and a 'Wiener Werkel', a typically Viennese barrel organ.

THE PIANO

Jazz pianist Oscar Peterson once said, 'Vienna is a piano town'. In the second half of the 18th century and in the 19th century, Vienna was indeed a major centre of piano manufacturing. Fortepianos are important forms of entertainment among the middle classes and their manufacture is a significant economic factor. The piano has maintained its place in the concert hall to this day.

The Piano-Maker's Workshop

Around 1700 in Florence, Bartolomeo Cristofori developed the first useable pianoforte from multiple-manual harpsichords. Until the beginning of the 19th century, pianos were built in piano makers' workshops. Manufacturing methods changed, however, because of the great demand, and in the first quarter of the 19th century, workshops that supplied piano parts developed in piano-making centres. Large-scale piano manufacturers concentrated production in factories and organised them under the principle of division of labour.

In the second half of the 19th century, this development led to improvements in efficiency and the standardization of piano models so that serial production became a possibility. More machines were used, metal parts like the frame and the strings strung across it were bought in.

Although computer-controlled machines are now used in piano making, the quality of a first-rate piano still depends on the skills and experience of a good piano maker with a distinctive idea of sound. No machine can ever replace his skills.

Fortepiano maker's workshop

Fortepiano by Anton Walter & Son, c. 1813. Inv. No. 35.240

The Forerunner of the Fortepiano

With strings plucked by a quill plectrum, harpsichords and spinets give a bright sound. The player's touch, however, cannot influence the volume of sound they produce – unlike the clavichord in which a metal pin (a tangent) produces a louder or softer sound depending on the force of the player's touch.

Owing to changing musical tastes in the 18th century, there was greater demand for a gradual transition between soft and loud sounds, one that the player could influence. The harpsichord was thus supplanted by the growing interest in the clavichord. Instrument makers were all the while seeking new ways in which to influence volume. Of the methods that they tried (invention of the Pantaleon and the clavichord, combinations of stringed pianos and small organs etc), only the pianoforte caught on. Its hammers could strike its strings both softly and loudly – piano and forte, in other words.

The Growth of Piano Making in Vienna

Piano making in Vienna quickly developed into an important industry. In the first thirty years of the 19th century, more than 380 piano and organ makers worked in the city. Smaller workshops often lasted no more than a generation; others lasted into the 20th century.

Even at the beginning of the 19th century, factory-like businesses and independent sub-contractors existed alongside craftsmen's workshops. Numerous patents – called 'privileges' in Vienna – reflect the inventiveness of the city's piano makers, especially in the ways they further developed the fortepiano. Come the end of the 19th century, it was a powerful instrument that could make itself heard even in large venues.

The exemplars of the instrument displayed here are by Walter, Streicher, Kober, Graf and Bösendorfer.

The Piano and the Bourgeoisie

In Austria, the bourgeoisie became the most important patrons of musical culture during the 'Biedermeier' era – roughly the period from 1815–48. People made music in their salons and, since the 're-discovery' of nature, outside too.

As the bourgeois salon was smaller than the aristocratic banqueting hall, space-saving pianos were invented, for instance the square piano whose keyboard is arranged parallel to its strings, or the various types of attractively embellished 'upright' pianos with vertical strings. For music making outside, there was the small, portable 'Orphica' as well as bowed string and wind instruments to be used as walking utensils.

The piano was often used to instil discipline in young children and adolescents who learned virtues such as diligence, orderliness and perseverance from practicing it. It was in this context that the piano also became an important status symbol.

Player Pianos: The Past is Alive

Self-playing pianos have existed since about 1840. Initially, the keys were struck by barrels with pins ('Planchetten') and perforated paper ribbons that acted as the 'data medium'. Later, the use of air pressure or vacuum ('pneumatic action') provided a much more precise action. The keys were struck by bellows activated by an air supply. Rows of perforations in a paper strip controlled the airflow.

Steinway-Welte player piano, 1913–15.
Inv. No. 29.244

Hupfeld's 'Phonoliszt Violina', the 'Eighth Wonder of the World', c. 1913. Inv. No. 7.457

Because other technically satisfying sound recordings from that era hardly exist, perforated paper strips from the early 20th century are valuable historical records of musical interpretation as they authentically reproduce the playing of famous pianists and composers such as Max Reger, Eugen d'Albert and Emil von Sauer.

The full range of products by the renowned German manufacturer Welte is on display as is a contemporary, electronically controlled counterpart, the 'disk piano'.

Piano and Violin: Two Instruments – One Machine

Player pianos quickly established themselves as a form of entertainment in bourgeois salons and inns, and this prompted a desire to combine them with other instruments such as accordions, for instance. Piano and violin combinations are particularly interesting because violins are the instruments least suited to mechanization. Nevertheless, Hupfeld's 'Violina' imitates the violin rather well by using three instruments and a curved bow that rotates at different speeds.

In a simpler version called the 'Violano Virtuoso', small celluloid wheels make the strings sound. The simplest and most robust design was the 'Weber Unica' whose special organ pipes produced violin-like sounds. All these instruments were controlled using perforated paper strips and had a large repertory of available titles.

Musical Instruments 145

Automatons and Apparatus: Music with and without Interpreters

Evidence of mechanical musical instruments has existed since the 17th century. At first, they were small flute clocks to which moving figures were later added. Since the 19th century, musical boxes with metal combs have been predominant. The great variety of instruments with barrels, metal or cardboard discs, paper and cardboard strips as the sound recording medium came to an abrupt end with the advent of the record.

Conventional instruments were also mechanized. The fiddle, for instance, was given a keyboard (Nyckelharpa) and a wheel replaced the bow to create a new instrument, the hurdy-gurdy. The zither and trumpet also had mechanical attachments.

Symphonium Eroica. Comb playing movement with 3 synchronised disks. Inv. No. 36.035

The Violin

Violin making first flourished in northern Italy during the 16th century when it developed a shape that it has retained to this day. Violins are still hand-made using the same materials as then. In German-speaking countries, lute makers, who had previously made string instruments, increasingly turned to violin making in the 18th century. By the 19th century, they had become 'makers of violins and guitars'.

Jakob Stainer from Absam in Tyrol is regarded as the founder of the violin making tradition north of the Alps. Many violin makers in southern Germany and Austria modelled their instruments on his.

The main tools and stages in violin making are shown in the violin-making workshop. The materials, parts and stages needed to restore a viola da gamba are also on display.

Violin maker's workshop

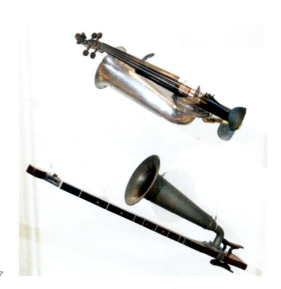

*Special types of violin: two Stroh violins from the 1920s with resonators for increased sound radiation.
Inv. Nos. 60.146, 60.147*

Wind Instruments

Wind instruments are among the oldest instruments in the world's cultures. In Nuremberg, for example, the activities of brass instrument makers were regulated as early as 1625. The city's trumpet makers were the best in Europe during the 17th and 18th centuries. Initially, brass instruments could produce only a few notes, but after 1814 valves that were developed in Vienna, among other places, succeeded in closing the gaps in the natural harmonic series.

Wood turners were the first main makers of woodwind instruments. As the 19th century progressed, more keys were added to produce an even sound quality.

Viennese Orchestral Horns and Oboes very much created their own distinctive sound.

Wind instrument maker's workshop

Miniature wind instruments in a chest of drawers

Success and Failure in Instrument Making

Instrument makers are not as conservative as is often claimed. Their modifications large and small, new designs and inventions have continually produced new designs and sound effects. Electronics widens the range of sound in quite amazing ways and experiments with unconventional keyboards or sensors. It is now easy to use the right instruments for music of disparate styles and eras or to experiment in new ways.

New or Reproduction?

Changes in musical tastes and instrument makers' love of experimentation have constantly given rise to new instruments as well as the development of existing ones. Besides improvements, however, mistakes have also been made. The Jankó keyboard was an attempt at an ergonomic, key-neutral keyboard that failed to find favour with musicians. Synthetic parts in instruments proved not to be long-lasting.

'New designs' were not always really new. Instrument makers often fell back on long-established or forgotten principles, as exemplified by the bowed keyboard, or 'Streichklavier', whose strings were bowed rather than struck, a principle that was already known in the 17th century.

Experimental keyboards: the Jankó keyboard. Inv. No. 32.163

The Advent of Electronics in Music

In the 1930s, instrument makers began to use electronic components for the new sounds they provided. Friedrich Trautwein and Lev Termen used electronic valves that had only just been invented to produce vibrations and built much-acclaimed instruments (the 'trautonium' and 'theremin vox'). They were the precursors of synthesizers and electronic organs that were widely used in light music and which were demonstrated to the public in 'electric concerts' at Berlin's Radio Exhibitions after 1931. Other predecessors of electronic instruments include those with metal rotating discs and magnetic sensors (Hammond Organ) as well as those with celluloid discs and optical sensors.

There are two main thrusts in the development of electronic instruments: on the one hand, instrument makers try to imitate conventional instruments in a true-to-life manner, mainly using computer technology; on the other hand, new sounds encourage composers to compose in new ways. Because the price of electronic instruments has fallen greatly, it is hard to imagine contemporary musical life without them.

The 'Theremin'. Inv. No. 50.336

SOUND AND SOUND RESEARCH

Sound research plays an important role not only in music, but in industry and medicine too. Vibrations in machines, hard disks or car doors, for instance, are investigated using the same means as in violins or piano sound-boards. Sound, especially ultrasound, plays an important role in medicine, for instance in imaging techniques that use ultrasonic scanners and in measurements of bone density. The exhibition contains selected examples of equipment used in sound research in the past and present. In a very simple way, the 'cylindrical oscilloscope' reveals the

The 'Mixturtrautonium'. Inv. No. 50.634

vibration pattern of strings, while an experiment with organ pipes permits slow-motion observation of the movement of air in the lips where sound is produced.
DoP

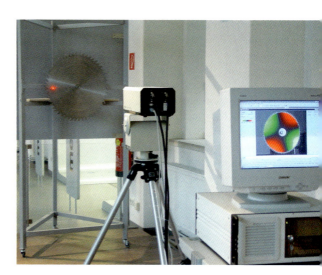

Using a laser vibrometer to scan a vibrating circular saw

Transport

Transport

Model of a Tyrolean flatboat. Inv. No. 18.389

An interactive terminal offering a panorama of the historical, technological and economic development of transport marks the start of 'Transport'. Means of transport and traffic routes are fundamental to traffic. Ships, lorries, cars, trains and planes are specific means of transport designed for conveyance by water, land and air.

Shipping

Boats are the oldest type of vehicle known to man. They were, and still are, not only a means of transport. For thousands of years, they were used mainly for fishing and trading; eventually they permitted great voyages of discovery across the world and allowed the transport of passengers. Buoys indicate the entrance to the exhibition on 'Shipping' and, at sea, act as navigation marks.

Rowing Boats

The dugout is among the earliest watercraft, and today's surfboard is a modern variation of it. Planks were added to the sides of dugouts to raise their height and were secured using frames. Pioneering the use of the keel around 800 AD, the Vikings created magnificent longships.

The rowing boats used here were flat-bottomed; side walls were fastened at right angles by means of ribs (frames). The joints between individual planks were V-shaped and were stopped up (caulked) using moss. Depending on how they were to be used, barges of different sizes were built; flatboats are an example.

Rafts – floated trees, boards, timber or logs – were needed. The 'Trauner' was a special type of Austrian boat that carried salt from the Salzkammergut region to the Danube. So-called 'salt convoys' plied the upper Danube; at Passau, the salt was transferred into larger vessels (called 'Kelheimer' and 'Gamsen') that were lashed together to form a train of vessels that was then hauled by 60–80 horses upriver to Regensburg. The cargo amounted to around 300 tons of salt. Nowadays, a barge carries 10,000 tons and more.

Sport Boats

Sport boats are represented by three types of craft in the exhibition: a 1930s collapsible boat, a 'Sea-Doo' built by the Austrian company Bombardier-Rotax and a dinghy of the 'Optimist' class in which children learn to sail. It may be a simple box, but it has everything you need to learn to sail!

Shipbuilding

Shape and stability are crucial to a ship's performance. The most important factor is a hydrodynamic hull. This problem was addressed by Austrian Fritz Maier who in 1905 received his first patent for the solution he devised. With his hull design, water resistance was about 20 per cent less than with conventional designs.

Seasickness is caused mainly by a ship's rolling motion along its longitudinal axis. The easiest way to reduce this motion is to build bilge keels along the ship's hull below the waterline. Gyro-controlled stabilisers are even more effective at reducing rolling.

The oldest method of propelling ships is probably the use of oars for rowing and steering. When steam engines were first fitted in ships, they powered paddle wheels. An Austrian forestry official called Josef Ressel

Model of Ressel's experimental ship 'Civetta', 1829. Inv. No. 17.863

used the Archimedes screw as a ship propulsion device. He was the first to position one in the most effective location on a ship, at the stern between the stern post and the rudder. In 1829, the experimental ship *Civetta* travelled a short distance in Trieste harbour before a soldered joint cracked and the experiment had to be abandoned. Although a competitor then had further experiments with the ship's screw banned, its success was unstoppable. Ressel had trained as a forester in Maria Brunn near Vienna and on postings to Istria, Venice and Trieste, he designed mills, stage machinery, a steam-powered vehicle and worked on the reforestation of karst areas.

An Austrian engineer called Ernst Leo Schneider, in collaboration with J. M. Voith Engineers in St. Pölten and Heidenheim (Württemberg), developed a new ship-propulsion device that combined propulsion and steering. Using two Voith-Schneider propellers, a ship can be steered in any direction from a stationary position. The first such propeller was fitted in the Danube tug *Uhu* in 1930. The model of the water tractor *Gnom* shows a boat with this type of propulsion device.

Mariners use knots that are easily untied even when a coil of rope is wet and swollen. The figure eight knot, for instance, holds well when

Voith-Schneider propulsion. Model of the water tractor 'Gnom', 1961. Inv. No. 33.246

pulled and is undone merely by placing the two ends together. When seamen tie the ends of two ropes together, they 'splice' them in a way that does not increase the width of the ropes.

Model Lighthouse and the Fresnel Lens

Lighthouses in antiquity made use of open fires. To make weak light visible from afar, curved reflectors or glass lenses were used to concentrate beams of light horizontally. As lenses became too large and too heavy, Frenchman Augustin Jean Fresnel in 1820 perfected an assemblage of separate concentric rings, which greatly reduced lens weight.

Austrian Lloyd

The Austrian Lloyd was established by Trieste-based insurers in 1832 as a steam navigation company. Scheduled services began in 1837. A model of one of its first vessels, the paddle steamer *Conte Stürmer*, is on display. Initially, Austrian Lloyd ships sailed to ports in the Mediterranean, especially the Adriatic; when the Suez Canal opened, scheduled services operated to India and as far as China.

Austrian Lloyd's shipyard was in Trieste where its ships were repaired in dry docks and new ones were built. A model of the *Oreste* shows the construction of an early steam ship: fitted with a propeller, the vessel still has sailing ship rigging that allowed it to save coal in favourable winds. Another model shows one of the last new constructions for Austrian Lloyd, the 112-meter-long twin-screw steamship *Gablonz* from 1912. Together with her sister ship, *Marienbad*, she sailed between Trieste and Bombay. One of the twin engines from the express steamer *Wien* is on display next to the model of the *Gablonz*. The *Wien's* engines were driven by steam produced by burning heavy oil in large boilers inside the hull. Models of her bridge and steam-powered steering system are also on display.

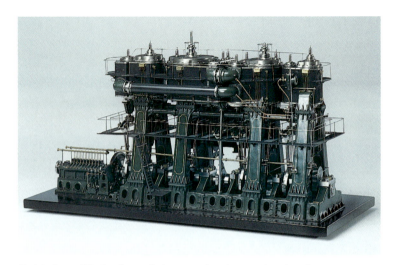

Model of one of the two four-cylinder expansion steam engines from the express steamer 'Wien', 1910. Inv. No. 1.619

Power-Driven Shipping on the Danube

'Transport' opens with a classic example of a side-wheeler with a dumb barge. Given normal water levels, up to four such barges could be towed on the upper reaches of the Danube; on the river's lower reaches, where the current is much less powerful, the number was twelve and more. A train of barges of this type needed a crew of ten to twelve. Push tows can be connected by rods to container barges, thus reducing the number of crew on the barges and bringing down wage costs.

Diesel-powered goods barges are the latest development and are manned by only two captains. Rationalisation on Europe's inland waterways means that smaller crews now transport increased tonnages. A century or so ago, it took a crew of thirty to transport four goods barges.

Vessels that were specially built for the Danube include the sternwheeler Temesvar that was suitable for use in shallow sections of the river, and the cable vessel *Nyitra*. Models of both are on display. Between 1869 and 1901, wire ropes or chains were let onto the bed of the Danube to allow low-powered vessels to transport heavy loads upriver.

Early passenger steamers on the Danube resembled sea-going vessels. Nowadays screw-driven passenger ships over 100 metres in length ply the river.

KeR

Road Traffic

The Bicycle
An early form of the bicycle was the draisienne, a machine propelled by the rider pushing against the ground. One manufactured by the Viennese firm of Anton Burg (*c.* 1820) is on display. The self-propelled concept was further developed at the onset of the 1860s in the Michaux bicycle from France and then, around 1880, in the 'penny farthing'. The difficulty of mounting the high seat was greatly reduced by the introduction of the 'safety bike'. The bicycle in its present form emerged during the 1890s. Pneumatic tyres and gears were especially significant developments. The Steyr 'Waffenrad' (*c.* 1900) was an Austrian favourite thanks to its sturdiness and was often inherited over several generations. It was still being built until recently almost unchanged.

The Motorbike
The motorbike left its experimental stage behind around 1900 with the start of large-scale production of the Laurin & Klement or the Puch with its sidecar. These were the first usable means of transport at the start of the age of motorized leisure time. After World War I, the British motorcycle industry was pre-eminent and its mid-range products dominated the

Puch 5 HP and sidecar, 1907–08. Inv. No. 7.558

Austrian market for want of domestic manufacturers. Top-range products, usually including a sidecar, were the preserve of the Americans with their Indians and Harley-Davidsons. After World War II, the motorbike found a place as a cheaper alternative to the car. When the post-war boom finally enabled large sections of society to buy a car – a 'roof over their head' – interest in the motorbike was confined to those with a sporting interest in it. Motorbikes were almost impossible to sell after 1960. It was not until the 1970s that they re-gained their original status as wheels for people out for a good time.

The Car
Pioneers of the Car
Gottlieb Daimler and Carl Friedrich Benz undoubtedly laid the foundation for today's mass motorization. Numerous engineers and inventors before them had experimented widely, but Daimler and Benz were the first to produce a commercially successful vehicle. The 'Benz Viktoria' from 1893 was the first car to be manufactured in large numbers for sale. When it became obvious that car manufacture was a lucrative business, several carriage builders in Austria like the Nesselsdorf Coach Factory and engineering works did what they could to secure their share of the market. Many newcomers with plenty of good will, but too little cash, failed. It was intended early on to build cheap cars that everybody could afford, a plan that was not realized in Europe until the mid-1930s. In America, Ford's Model T heralded the start of mass motorization after the end of World War I.

Alternative Forms of Propulsion around 1900
While the petrol engine was crucial to the success of the motorcar at the start of the 1890s, it still had a number of technological shortcomings. Alternatives to it were electric and steam drive.

The advantages of electric drive were that it was quiet, clean and easy to use; its disadvantages were the weight of batteries and low storage capacity – a problem in electric vehicles that has still to be solved satisfactorily. Under certain conditions, nonetheless, electric drive can still be the best solution. When Americans landed on the Moon, they used

Lohner-Porsche, 1900
Inv. No. 1.428

electric vehicles with wheel hub motors as manufactured by Lohner-Porsche. In towns and cities, too, there are often benefits in using electric drive, for instance in parcel delivery or factory vehicles.

Where the steam-driven motorcar scored was in its robust method of construction and range, advantages known from locomotive construction. Steam engines had to be adapted to the motorcar's special requirements and operating conditions, however. The downside to the steam-driven motorcar lay in the length of time it needed to be up and running, the necessity for complicated adjustments and its unwieldiness. Besides, the petrol engine developed rapidly, thus obviating the need for alternatives.

Austrian Cars

The beginning of the history of car manufacture in Austria was characterized by pioneering technical achievements. Many years before Daimler and Benz, Siegfried Marcus appears to have been the first to use the successful combination of petrol as fuel and electric ignition. Before 1900, the 'Gebrüder Gräf' designed a front-wheel drive car of the most up-to-date design. They were so far ahead of their time that it failed to sell and it remained the only one of its kind.

After 1900, nevertheless, the car industry in Austria was internationally respected. Some of the leading makes were Austro-Daimler and Gräf

'Marcuswagen'
Inv. No. 1.404

& Stift – the favourite of the Austrian royal family and aristocracy. The Duke of Cumberland drove the car that is on display. Few makes survived World War I. Feeling the pressure of the economic crisis, car factories were forced to cut back on development costs and to manufacture cheap models. Notwithstanding these difficulties, Gräf & Stift, Austro-Daimler and Steyr continued to produce models that could bear international comparison. Numerous racing victories in the inter-war years also proved the competitiveness of the Austrian car industry. Its good reputation was based more on its robust domestic products, however. The Steyr 220 cabriolet captivated drivers not only with its efficient technology but also with its timeless design. The Steyr 55 'Baby' really was a 'people's car' before the advent of the Volkswagen (literally 'people's car'). For the first time, advertising targeted women as potential customers. Germany's annexation of Austria in 1938 cut short its success. After World War II, Austria's car industry largely restricted itself to supplying components – except for the manufacture of the small Puch 500. A cluster of internationally successful firms has developed in Graz since the 1970s and 1980s.

Motor Racing
Racing with road vehicles is almost as old as road vehicles themselves. The first 'Semmering' race was held in 1900. From the start, Austrian manufacturers and drivers participated in motor racing. The 'Celeritas' vehicle that is on display is the oldest extant Austrian racing car. A long line of Austrians has played and still plays an important part in international motor racing, stretching from Ferdinand Porsche to Alfred Neubauer (race organizer with Mercedes) to Jochen Rindt, Niki Lauda and Gerhard Berger. One of the highlights of the Museum's motorcar display, the Mercedes 'Silberpfeil', dominated the 1954 and 1955 racing seasons.

Motor racing was and still is very popular in Austria. In the inter-war years, it had more followers than football. The Austrian motorcycle man-

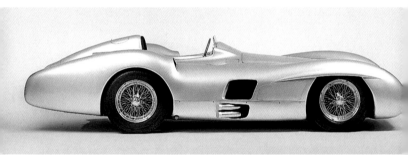

Mercedes W 196 'Silberpfeil', 1954–55. Inv. No. 16.798

ufacturer Puch was similarly committed to the sport. Despite numerous successes, including ones on the international circuit, the company frequently had to withdraw from international racing for lack of funds.
ScG

The Railways

The combination of wheels and rails to form rail traffic greatly increased haulage capacity in mines as long ago as the Middle Ages. A crucial milestone in the development of the first efficient land-based transport system was the availability of steam power as a source of propulsion. It created the prerequisites for an industrialized society at the start of the 19th century in England, the birthplace of the railway.

The railway era in Austria began in 1832 with the opening of the horse-drawn railway between Linz and Budweis. Only the passenger carriage 'Hannibal' has survived; it is unique in the world. The transition to steam power was made in 1837 on the Kaiser Ferdinand Northern Line from Vienna to Cracow with a train pulled by 'Austria', the locomotive whose model is displayed here.

Passenger carriage 'Hannibal' from the Linz-Budweis horse-drawn railway, built 1841. The first carriages and, later, locomotives were names after cities, famous men in antiquity etc. Inv. No. E-77

This new means of transport, in whose development 'Austria' played a significant role, was a great challenge to engineers, bankers and industrialists. Carl Ritter von Ghega deserves special mention here: he built the world's first mountain railway across the Semmering pass between 1848–54.

Line construction is basic railway technology. On display is a 95-cm-long cast-iron fish-bellied rail from the horse-drawn railway between Linz and Budweis. It illustrates just how far the railway has come since then to today's high speed trains travelling along long-welded rails.

Imperial saloon car HZ 0011 used by Empress Elisabeth, built in 1873. Interior view. Inv. No. 40.331

'Vindobona' steam engine on the Kaiser-Ferdinand Northern Line. Built 1837, England. This model, made in 1843, is a particular rarity. Inv. No. E-5

River crossings and advances into mountainous terrain placed new demands on bridge builders and led to the development of tunnel construction. On display is a model of a wooden bridge that illustrates the early design of structural members with the load-bearing capacity required for the railway. The legendary steel construction of the Trisanna Bridge on the Arlberg line clearly shows how much progress was made in the 15 years that separate the two designs. Austria to this day remains at the forefront of tunnel construction.

Carl Ritter von Ghega built the world's first mountain railway across the Semmering pass, 1848–54. Inv. No. 22.366

Suitable vehicles also had to be built. It is obvious from the Northern Line carriages, but most especially from Hannibal, that railway carriages initially borrowed from coach building. It was not long, however, before coachbuilders switched to box construction types, with compartments accessed either from the side doors or by passageways connecting compartments, the system still used today and illustrated by the coaches from the Vienna-Gloggnitz railway. Improvements were made over time to the levels of comfort enjoyed by passengers; they ranged from the addition of suspension to coach bodies (they initially lacked any!) to heating and lighting to the installation of toilets around 1870. Saloon cars, and more so imperial saloon cars, were comfortably and lavishly equipped. The saloon car built for Empress Elisabeth in 1873 is a truly exclusive exhibit; after being restored, it will be on show on the Museum's ground floor.

The crucial innovation, however, was the invention of the steam locomotive that was first used to haul a train in 1804 in Britain. The first steam-powered railway opened in 1829 between Liverpool and Manchester. George Stephenson's Rocket had won a locomotive competition and had all the features of later locomotives. In keeping with its role as a leading centre of locomotive construction, Britain supplied all the railways that were then being developed, including those in Austria. Besides Austria (mentioned above) there was also Vindobona, a model of which was built by an engine driver on the Northern Line in 1843 (!). It really is rather special as it is the oldest model in the collection.

Austria first began to build locomotives in 1840 and made important contributions to their development. The designer Karl Gölsdorf gained a worldwide reputation for constructing 25 basic models from which 47 series were developed. He designed the locomotives for Vienna's steam-powered city railway that were in use until 1925. One of the series, still in working order, is on display at Strasshof Railway Museum, an outstation of the Technisches Museum Wien, that currently houses 48 locomotives and 31 other vehicles including the famous BBÖ 310.23 steam locomotive – again Gölsdorf's design and still in working order.

The monarchy's first electric railway was put into service in 1883 between Mödling and Hinterbrühl, south of Vienna. Europe's first alternating current railway followed in 1904 – its motor, a world first, is on display – and in 1912 the monarchy's first standard gauge railway opened, both in Tyrol.

When Austria lost its coal reserves after World War I, greater effort was put into constructing electric railways such as the Arlbergbahn. Because power requirements could not be met from the existing network, the country's hydropower potential had to be tapped and power stations for the use of the railways had to be built, including the Spullersee power station that opened in 1925. Suitable electric locomotives were built at the same time. Krokodil, built after 1923, has become a legend. A model of it is on display here, the original is at Strasshof Railway Museum. After the 1930s, combustion-driven locomotives came into use for the first time, especially as railcars. With the exception of a few narrow gauge and mountain railways like the Schafberg railway, no steam-powered railways have run in Austria since 1977. Electric traction is now used on all main routes.

Of the installations needed to operate a railway, it is railway stations that passengers mainly come into contact with. After modest beginnings, they developed into splendid buildings. The model of Vienna's second Northern Station that was destroyed in World War II illustrates the point.

Another pillar of railway operations is safety technology that likewise has developed over a long period of time. Because trains have long stopping distances, driving by sight is not possible, nor can evasive action be taken. This means that special installations are needed to allow stations to communicate with train crews travelling between them. Originally, time spacing was used to run trains: by means of optical signals, signalmen monitored passing trains, but this system proved unworkable. It was superseded by a system based on a minimum distance that was equal to the stopping distance of trains; this was the minimum distance that had to be kept between trains. This led to the introduction of stop and distant signals that are closely associated with signal boxes as established after 1870. They allowed signals to be set and fixed using remote control or independently of the points.

An exhibition of signal boxes and signals is currently being installed at Strasshof Railway Museum.

Information was transmitted to signalmen or between stations at first using an optical telegraph like the basket signal that was also used to signal to trains. Austria's first electric railway communications system opened in 1845. It was followed in 1856 by electric bell signals, by Morse code around mid-century and by the telephone in 1879.

Nowadays, centralized traffic control (CTC) covers whole stretches of track and is an important element of efficient railway management. Computers have now been used for years to ensure safety; in conjunction with continuous automatic train control, as in the case of Vienna's Underground, they continuously transmit information or instructions to trains.

Trams and underground trains are an important feature of urban traffic. A number of models illustrate the development of Vienna's trams, the first of which started in 1865 and were horse-drawn. The system was electrified from 1897 onwards.

Austria's topography and increasing recreational use of its mountainous areas resulted in the construction of rack mountain railways, cableways and other means of ascent. Both Austria and Switzerland are leaders in the field. The world's first passenger cableway was the Kohlernbahn near Bolzano (South Tyrol) that opened in 1908. During renovations in 1913, gondolas were added that were essentially the same as today's designs. The model on display illustrates the point nicely.

The number of cableways in Austria today is indicative of their economic importance: 805 cable railways, including the funicular railways at Salzburg and Graz, and 2,384 lifts of various types.

The railways are now restructuring because they are in competition with road traffic that in some respects is more efficient, but in view of environmental considerations, railways can be expected to remain an important feature of the transport system.
KnK

Uniform worn by a superintendent of the Imperial Austrian Railways, 1891 issue. Inv. No. E-68

Aviation

To conquer the air was a long-held dream of mankind's. Aviation first began with the use of balloons and airships. The flight of birds served as a model, and the construction of suitable engines eventually led to the development of aircraft. Life today is unimaginable without this means of transport.

Otto Lilienthal flying a small gliding bi-plane, 1895

Balloons and Airships

In France at the end of the 18th century, the Montgolfier brothers discovered that hot air rises. The two paper mill owners then set about making paper balloons and filled them with hot air. The 21 November 1783 saw the first human ascents into the air, and on 1 December 1783 the first balloon filled with hydrogen gas, built by J.A.C. Charles, lifted off the ground. The spell was broken.

At the close of the 19th century, the military used captive balloons to observe the enemy and, during World War I, used barrage balloons as anti-aircraft defences. Civilians also came to enjoy the new perspective of the Earth from the air: around 1900 the wealthy classes and some artists discovered ballooning as a new pastime and sport. The depression during the inter-war years also affected ballooning, however. After World War II, the development of simple petroleum and gas burners for hot-air balloons transformed ballooning into a popular aerial sport that still has a hint of luxury attached to it.

In a balloon, man is at the mercy of the wind. To steer towards a particular point, a motor with propellers is needed. In 1852, French aviation pioneers, with little success, attempted to fly a steam-powered non-rigid airship. The gas engine invented by Jean Lenoir in 1860 raised new hopes. Paul Haenlein tested an airship fitted with a Lenoir engine in Brünn/Brno in 1872. After 1900, the guided airship embarked on a triumphant progress that is associated with Ferdinand Graf Zeppelin. His design of a rigid frame enclosing gas bags for lifting power and impulse proved its mettle and the first scheduled passenger flights started in Germany in 1906. World War I further improved airship technology and large-scale production was started. As aircraft at the time did not have the range of airships, the first trans-Atlantic passenger service was started by the LZ.127 Graf Zeppelin. The technology suffered a huge setback when the LZ.129 Hindenburg burst into flames while landing at Lakehurst, New Jersey in 1937. There are proposals to build new airships capable of carrying heavy loads in future.

Aviation Pioneers

Otto Lilienthal was the most important of the many pioneers of flight. He first observed storks, measured their wings and then constructed an apparatus that allowed him to determine the resistance and lift exerted on surfaces. On the strength of his findings, Lilienthal built several gliders, and in 1891, he made the first flight in one of them. Five years later, however, he was killed in a crash while carrying out further tests. The Museum has in its collection one of the few remaining Lilienthal originals, the 'Sturmflügel' from 1894.

Other aviation theoreticians took their lead from Lilienthal's singlemindedness. Among them were the Austrians Friedrich von Lössl, whose aerodynamic weighing machine is on display, and Georg Wellner and Richard Knoller, who built the first atmospheric pressure open-jet wind tunnel. Ernst Mach (Mach number indicating the speed of sound) and Christian Doppler (Doppler effect) elaborated important physical principles that would be applied in air travel.

After 1877 in Austria, Wilhelm Kress built the first self-starting, self-propelled and self-landing model planes pushed on by rubber strings. In 1900–01 Kress attempted to build a large 'Drachenflieger' (triplane

Original model of an aircraft built by Wilhelm Kress, 1877. Inv. No. 1.922

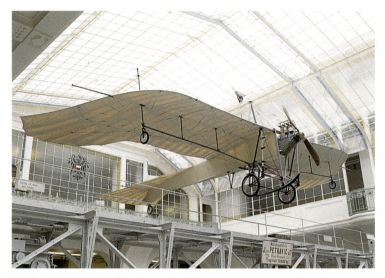

The first Etrich-II 'Taube' (Dove), 1910. Inv. No. 1.933

winged aircraft). The world's first petrol-engine-powered float plane, it sank while being tested on an artificial lake in the Vienna Woods. Kress' ideas about aircraft capable of vertical takeoff were realised, but not until much later.

The American brothers Wilbur and Orville Wright also first experimented with gliders and studied lift before their first powered flights were successful in 1903. In Austria at the same time, father and son Ignaz and Igo Etrich were experimenting with wing designs and after countless tests found their answer in a tropical windblown seed, Zanonia macrocarpa. On display is an Etrich-II 'Taube' (Dove) that took its name from the dovetail added to it to stabilize powered flight. After 1907, many aviation pioneers across the world helped to advance the technology needed for powered flight. Based on their efforts, a military aircraft industry

Austro-Daimler AD 12. First 12-cylinder-V-Motor from Austria-Hungary, 1914. Inv. No. 1.858

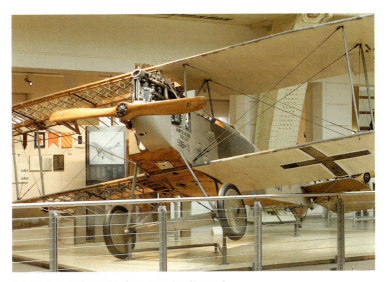
Aviatik-Berg D I fighter bi-plane, 1918. Inv. No.1.916

developed during World War I that led to the mass production of aircraft. An original Aviatik-Berg D I bi-plane symbolising the fighter plane of its era is on display. This was the first Austrian fighter plane to be mass-produced. The navy used flying boats and float planes.

Several aircraft engines from the pioneering days of aviation are on display including the first Austrian twelve-cylinder engine from 1914 as designed by Ferdinand Porsche.

Towards Commercial Aviation

After the war, any remaining military aircraft were used to convey mail and passengers. The first passenger aircraft, such as the Junkers F-13, were built in the 1920s.

A model of Aspern airport outside Vienna reveals how aviation had developed by the mid-1930s and the types of single-engine and triple-engine all-metal Junkers aircraft that were used. Aerial sports had modest beginnings. In Austria, Theodor Hopfner and Erich Meindl built several types of aircraft, including, in 1939, Germany's first aircraft with a nose wheel.

The large numbers of four-engine bombers and transporters that were built during World War II provided the technological prerequisites for the trans-Atlantic passenger aircraft that were developed after 1945. Jet engines, also developed by the military, halved flying time. Wide-bodied aircraft can cover huge distances and because the cost of flying has fallen, the airplane has become a means of mass transportation. New methods of production engineering and new materials combined with ongoing aerodynamic improvements have reduced fuel consumption per passenger kilometre.

KeR

The 'Mini'

An activities area for two to six-year-olds, the 'Mini' covers an area of about 350 m² on two levels and invites the Museum's youngest visitors to discover technology for the first time through play. The emphasis is not on conventional learning, however. Instead, youngsters are given the opportunity to 'grasp' hands-on exhibits and models appropriate to their age group in pleasant and light-filled surroundings, to train their powers of observation and to get involved in the Museum's activities. As they set about 'conquering' this indoor playground, the Museum's youngest visitors – and their parents – begin to appreciate the Museum as a cultural space of their own.

The self-contained educational units used in the 'Mini' encourage independent thought and action, and are intended to bring technology to 'life' using the principle of cause and effect. The 'Mini' is a reflection of the Museum itself: from the fields of physics and music, for instance, it contains objects dealing with optics, sound and vibrations; related to the 'Energy' exhibition, there are experiments on power transmission and aerodynamics. The exhibits in the 'Mini' allow hands-on activities and stimulate all five senses. Small temporary exhibitions are also held.

Fun with all the Senses

See things, hear things, touch things and *smell* things! Or how about skipping, sliding or building? Make a ball float in the air! Kids can try everything in the 'Mini'.

The 'Bernoulli Blower' appears to have dispensed with gravity by allowing balls to float freely in the air. Cogwheels illustrate the interaction between individual components in a mechanical system. Kids can operate the cogwheels themselves to understand how they have to engage to achieve an effect. The 'apple tree' encourages kids to feel around for hidden objects and to use their sense of smell. The 'touchy-feely wall' is designed to stimulate the senses and the imagination. By jumping up and down on the 'bouncy piano', kids can produce sounds and even play children's songs. Budding architects can give free reign to their imagination 'on site' using a crane and build their own house. Beforehand, they can produce their own technical drawings on a special computer. And for those who have always wanted to take a car to bits, the 'Mini's' garage beckons with a miniature Model T Ford. A real fire engine is there to be discovered and those who are strong enough can hoist themselves into the air using a block and tackle. The KidSmart computer has been designed with youngsters in mind and captures their imaginations with loads of things to learn.

The 'Mini' can be visited during Museum opening hours.
HaA, HaB

A real fire engine to climb on

Education at the Technisches Museum Wien

Experiencing technology through play at a 'camp-in'

'If the weather's bad, rather than go walking, we'd like to come to you. Do we need to book in advance?' Questions like this from teachers are now a thing of the past. In recent years, the Technisches Museum Wien has become well-known thanks to contentious debate about technological issues and its appealing education programme. More than ever before, it is now a museum that can be experienced with all the senses.

More than half of our visitors are teenagers or families. In addition, technophiles, interested laypersons, tourists and senior citizens come and visit us. The Technisches Museum Wien offers pleasant surroundings in which to consider questions about technology, the history of technology and the natural sciences. Many aspects of the history of technology are shown in a monumental building erected in the 1910s

Understanding technology as an individual visitor

where technology is examined as a complex cultural phenomenon. On the one hand, we display artefacts and explain the context in which they were originally used; on the other hand, hands-on exhibits offer visitors the chance to experience technology for themselves. This combination of seeing and doing allows visitors to gain some new knowledge and to ask questions about the advantages of scientific findings and technological applications. The Museum's education programme includes a wide range of options that allows visitors to relate to its exhibits. Depending on people's interests and the time they have available, there are different levels of text to provide orientation. More in-depth information can be found in file-card boxes, at multimedia stations or in the films shown in the various exhibition areas. This type of presentation

Marvel at technology

invites visitors to discover the Museum at their own pace and exploit its resources. By providing individual access in this way, the Museum also becomes a place of communication between visitors of different backgrounds and generations.

Established in 1990, the Museum's education section offers a broad education programme that takes the existing store of knowledge and the potential of different visitor groups as its starting point. Creative learning by doing is basically how it imparts knowledge. Discussing and questioning established thought patterns increases receptivity for new insights and experiences. Out-of-the-box-thinking – the slogan for the constant search for new ideas – and 'joined-up' thinking are central to the presentation of complex contexts.

As part of the Museum's refurbishment, besides a spacious entrance area with a shop, two spaces were created for undisturbed group activities. They offer creative scope for kids' birthday parties and the Museum's educational programmes.

Male and female instructors give visitors an understanding of topics using lively techniques that foster knowledge and intuition. Their creative approach to and examination of topics is tailored to the age group in question.

The services of education staff are available both for the Museum's collections and special exhibitions, with techniques appropriate to an exhibition's content. In addition, they run treasure hunts and take tours of the Museum's highlights that include the mine reconstruction, the high-voltage room, the gallery of steam engines and the Virtual-Reality Theatre. Teachers' resources and treasure hunts can be downloaded from our homepage.

A separate programme of tours is of course available to meet the special needs of visitors with disabilities.

In addition to these offers that are available in different forms for all age groups, we offer special holiday activities for kids such as our 'camp-in', a night spent in the Museum for which participants come prepared with a rucksack and sleeping bag. Combining fun and learning, birthday celebrations in the Museum are also a great experience.

Since 2004, we have had a special offer for schools. For a small fee, they can make regular use of the Museum for teaching purposes and include more visits to the Museum as part of lessons.

A visit to the Museum during the school holidays and above all on Christmas Eve has been an integral part of childhood for generations of Viennese that is recalled with affection decades later.

SzW, HaB

Archive and Library

The new Reading Room on level 5

As an information and documentation centre for the cultural history of technology, the Archive and Library in the Technisches Museum Wien form an important collection of source material and literature for scientific research. Their resources are unmatched in their diversity in Austria and are used both by Museum staff and outside researchers.

The Library and Archive house written material, images, sound recordings and electronic media relating to the natural sciences and the history of technology with a particular focus on Austria. Two instruments provide the organisational and legal framework: the 'Forschungsorganisationsgesetz' (FOG; Law on the Organisation of Research) and the 'Bundesgesetz über die Sicherung, Aufbewahrung and Nutzung von Archivgut des Bundes (Bundesarchivgesetz)' (Federal Law Relating to the Safeguarding, Storage and Use of Archive Materials owned by the Federal Government (Federal Archive Laws)). In addition there are regulations governing the Museum.

The Archive and Library have been integral to the concept of the Museum since its foundation. Even in his 1908 programme for the Technisches Museum, Wilhelm Franz Exner mentioned the operation and remit of a library and archive. For Exner, the establishment of a 'specialist technical library' and an archival collection relating to the history of technology were necessary complements to the collection of objects.

In line with their importance, the Library and Archive were originally to have been housed in generous accommodation in a separate admin-

Library's Reading Room, c. 1955

istrative building. Four years before the Museum opened, a room was modified as storage space for books and archive material and also included a reading area.

Library Collection

The Library currently holds over 100,000 volumes on the history of technology and its associated sciences, the history of trade and industry, biographies of engineers and scientists as well as technical literature. Special collections like the rare books collection and collections of world's fair and company catalogues essentially define the institution's unique status. This specialist library has been included in the 'Handbook of Historical Book Collections in Austria' published by the Austrian National Library.

All printed material published before 1800 belongs to the 'rare books' stock. Among the oldest works in the collection are *Der newen Perspec-*

Archive Depot

tiva das I. buch by Gualtherus H. Rivius, printed in Nuremberg in 1547, and a *Theatrum instrumentorum et machinarum* by Jacobus Bessonius from 1578. Besides Georgius Agricola's *De re metallica*, works by Jacob Leupold are also represented. Moreover, the Library possesses the *Encyclopédie, ou dictionnaire raisonné des sciences des arts et des métiers* as edited by Denis Diderot and Jean-Baptiste d'Alembert. Among the stock of technical encyclopaedias, Johann Georg Krünitz' *Ökonomisch-technologische Encyklopädie*, Johann Joseph Prechtl's *Technologische Encyklopädie oder alphabetisches Handbuch der Technologie, der technischen Chemie und des Maschinenwesens* and Karl Karmarsch's and Friedrich Herren's *Technisches Wörterbuch* are especially noteworthy. Furthermore, the Library holds items that were regarded as the most important reference works for industry and the factory system in Austria in the first half of the 19th century, Stephan Edler von Keess' *Darstellung des Fabriks- und Gewerbswesens im österreichischen Kaiserstaate* and the *Systematische Darstellung der neuesten Fortschritte in den Gewerben und Manufacturen*, again edited by Keess in conjunction with Wenzel Carl Wolfgang Blumenbach.

Among the Museum's treasures is a collection of catalogues from world fairs, starting with the one in Paris in 1855. With a total of 150 volumes, the event that was the Vienna world fair in 1873 is covered in great detail.

Another valuable Library asset is the collection of early product catalogues from around 1900 until the inter-war years. An important means of identifying products and machines, this collection is also used by companies researching their own history.

Readers can consult the annual volumes of specialist journals in the reading room. Among journals no longer printed, Ludwig Förster's *Allge-*

Catalogue of the Rudolf Schwarz company, Vienna

meine Bauzeitung, the *Allgemeine Automobilzeitung* and the *Österreichische Ingenieur- und Architekten-Zeitschrift* are worth mentioning.

Archive Collections

The archive in the Technisches Museum Wien contains a broad range of storage media: there are manuscripts, technical drawings, oil paintings, material produced using different printing processes, photographs, certificates, files and audio-visual media, to name only the most important. The diversity of the source material, especially the large number of images, constitutes the remarkable feature and significance of this collection that fills *c.* 1,300 m of shelf space.

The Collection of Manuscripts and Diplomas contains the manuscripts of important Austrian engineers and scientists, certificates, letters, manuscripts of lectures and lecture notes, patents, and diplomas, note books, diaries and manuscripts from a wide range of sources. The stock has 2,650 shelf marks and covers the period from the second half of the 16th century to the present.

In addition, the archive administers a collection of private papers from sixty-six estates of famous Austrian engineers, industrialists and businessmen. Josef Ressel, Alois Negrelli, Wilhelm Kress, Carl Auer von Welsbach, Ferdinand Redtenbacher, August Musger, Victor Kaplan, Gustav Tauschek, Erich Meindl and Johann Radinger are among those whose private papers are included partially in this collection.

The Collection of Images and Plans forms the historical core of the archive and includes plans, technical drawings, prints, photographs, etchings and product advertising. The Biographical Collection contains biographical information on 330 engineers and scientists and was established by the 'Österreichisches Forschungsinstitut für Geschichte der Technik' (Austrian Research Institute for the History of Technology).

So-called 'Frühakten' (early files) form a special collection among the administrative archive files. They not only document the history of the Museum's foundation, but also are a valuable source of information for companies researching their own history.

Among the 'Small and Special Stock', several items are worth mentioning: holdings on the Danube–Oder Canal, Luftfahrttechnische Dokumentation Molin (Molin Aeronautical Documentation Centre), ships' blueprints from Korneuburg shipbuilding yard, a collection of brochures about vehicles and their instructions for use, and the photographic record of Vienna's world fair.

Georgius Agricola, De re metallica, 1621

Maréchal Grossier (farrier). From: Diderot/d'Alembert, Encyclopédie…, Planches 1762–77

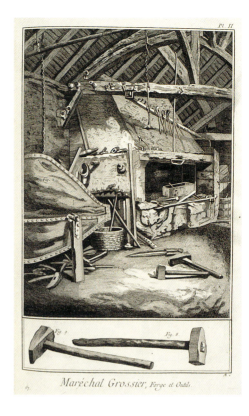

Moreover, the archive has a comprehensive 'Cartographical Collection' comprising around 2,500 postal route maps, telephone and telegraph charts, railway charts, city maps and other maps inherited from the former Post Museum.

The 'Photographic Collection' contains 100,000 items mostly in the form of negatives or transparencies on glass or synthetic plates. Their subject matter is mostly technical objects and people associated with the history of technology, but work processes and images of production sites are also found. Magic lantern slides showing images of merchandise knowledge are a peculiar feature of the Archive.

Infrastructure and Databases

The Library and Archive now make use of infrastructure tailored to the special requirements of the Museum's archivists and librarians: the long-term storage of source documents relating to the history of technology in centralised, air-conditioned storage rooms, the administration of these documents and their use in offices and hands-on rooms and their availability in the reading room.

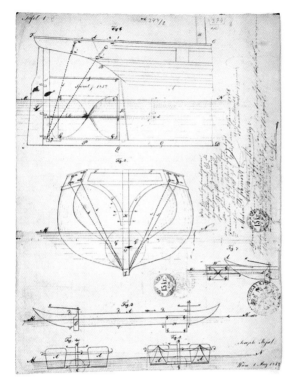

Josef Ressel, Archimedes screw positioned at the stern, 1812. Drawing

The new reading room accommodates twelve users who can consult the extensive Library and Archive collections undisturbed in individual reading bays. In addition, a worktable is available for large-scale archival material and can be used for group work. Reading room users have at their immediate disposal an extensive selection of biographical, encyclopaedic and specialist reference works. Research can be undertaken using the Online Public Access Catalogue (OPAC) of the library's database; the authors' and subject catalogues for older stock and by accessing the data pool of archive data integrated into the Museum's object database.

The Future

The adoption of multimedia databases and retrieval systems as well as new technologies and information systems has allowed the Museum to adapt to the basic requirements of today's information society. The Museum can thus fully exploit the potential of its collections and can participate actively in the information market and profit from it.

Besides collecting and conserving sources of information relating to the history of technology, it remains one of the Library and Archive

Steyr 50, c. 1936. Brochure

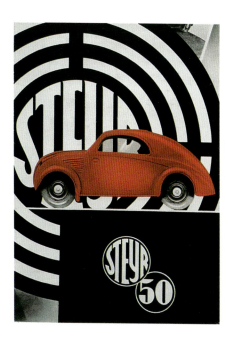

staff's key duties to evaluate such sources and to make them available. It is our aim to provide specialised and personal assistance to those in search of information on issues relating to the history of technology.
FeM, StH

Boiler plant. Photograph

The Conservation Section

There is a wide range of objects in the care of the museum's conservators: it goes from globes to aircraft engines and from portable radios to a crucible used in the LD (basic oxygen) process of steelmaking.

The museum's holdings usually come in a range of materials that requires in-depth knowledge of materials, scientific knowledge, skilled craftsmanship, an awareness of techniques used in the past as well as flexibility and sensitivity. By conserving the museum's assets, important sources of information are preserved for the present and future generations. When intervention is necessary, it should preferably be reversible; all conservation measures, whether reversible or not, must be meticulously documented. Yet in all intervention, whether necessitated by the requirements of exhibiting objects or questions of research, one thing

Textile conservators working in the Imperial saloon car

Cleaning of an object in the depot

must be kept in mind: the questions asked about the past and the aims behind exhibiting objects in museums change relatively quickly. To ensure that the information content of items is not lost forever merely for the sake of short-term aims, conservation measures must take priority each time.

Besides caring for the objects on display in the museum, the Conservation Section is also responsible for the items stored in the museum's large depots. The majority of objects held there present great challenges in terms of financial planning, logistics, correct storage, temperature control and pest control.

In recent years, most museums have experienced a surge in demand for loans of their holdings, a development that requires even greater involvement on the part of their conservators.
BrZ

Depots

Depot Breitensee, exterior view

Museums with a cultural and historical focus usually have around five to ten per cent of their collections on display to the public at any one time. The vast majority of items are kept in museum depots. Museums with large historical collections, such as the Technisches Museum Wien, very much also function as archives and repositories of history.

In the case of museums of industry and technology, the storage of three-dimensional objects represents a special challenge in that they can range from steel and iron machines weighing many tons to small and fiddly objects made of paper or fabric. Managers of the museum's stores, inventory administrators and restorers are the people mainly responsible for storing the museum's holdings.

On opening in May 1918, the Technisches Museum Wien had only the use of its loft for storage purposes. Given the constant lack of space, many an exhibition area also functioned as a storage-cum-exhibition space over the decades. When the museum closed temporarily in autumn 1992 and was cleared for refurbishment, its depot was decentralised across several locations. Besides the three buildings at its main depot in the district of Breitensee, for the duration of the closure the museum had stores at Hietzing, at Vienna's Northwest Station, at Schloss Niederweiden (Lower Austria) and in Siegendorf (Burgenland).

Once the museum re-opened in 1999, financial, organisational and conservation requirements meant that a solution to this awkward situation had to be found. Essentially, the aim was to concentrate the museum's holdings in a small number of depots within Vienna.

The former office building at Breitensee was converted into a depot that complied with fire safety requirements and became the new home for the items stored in Hietzing and Niederweiden. Designed by architect Robert Oerley and built during World War I, the listed five-storey, reinforced concrete Zeiss building was renovated next. The objects that had previously been stored there were returned. As part of its refurbish-

Depot Breitensee, interior view

ment, the building had a stacking system for the museum's collection of paintings installed. The paintings depot and three other rooms where the railway archive is held had previously had an air conditioning system installed.

To replace the depots at Vienna's Northwest Station, Siegendorf and Breitensee, which was again needed by the Austrian army's estates management section, the museum rented another depot in the district of Floridsdorf. It is a factory building that was once part of the Pauker Works and dates mainly from 1907.

The museum has thus achieved its goal of concentrating its depots at two locations in three buildings with a total of about 17,000 m² of storage space. Over four years, almost three million euros were invested in building work, fire safety measures, outfitting and warehouse logistics. To administer the 100,000 inventoried items in the museum's care, a new electronic database with links to the depots was also installed. A new inventory of all the items in the museum's depots was started in summer 2003.

LaH

Österreichische Mediathek:
The Austrian Multimedia Centre

As the national archive for audiovisual documents, the Österreichische Mediathek is home to a unique collection in which Austria's audiovisual heritage is documented, preserved and made available to interested members of the public.

Its holdings convey an image of the country's cultural and intellectual life, and reflect its eventful history. The main emphasis lies in the fields of music, literature and cabaret, politics and contemporary history as well as science and art. Video recordings of scenes from everyday life but also of unusual cultural and scientific events, filmed by a team from the Österreichische Mediathek, add to the extensive collection of over one million recordings.

Not only sounds, but sound carriers themselves provide a survey of over a century of media history. From self-cut lacquer discs and shellac disks to CDs and DVDs, the Österreichische Mediathek contains all

The Österreichische Mediathek's mass storage system

The Mediathek's location

kinds of sound carriers. Several collections are especially noteworthy: with over 80,000 items, the collection of 78s is the largest in Austria and contains numerous rarities, particularly musical ones; historic political speeches in relation to the country's history; rare, post-war radio recordings; recordings of debates in the 'Nationalrat'; and, not least, the music collection as a whole which not only contains over 6,000 recordings of the music of Mozart, but also a representative cross section of musical life in Austria today.

Audiovisual media are not durable, however, and for that reason the Österreichische Mediathek began to digitize its holdings in 2000. To this end, it developed a completely new system that can guarantee the preservation of its holdings. It is supported by a database based on the rules of academic libraries that ensures the optimum administration of documents as well as a mass storage archival system.

The task of digitizing is carried out using special computer workstations that allow analogue to digital conversion and create high-resolution wav files (96 kHz / 24 bit). In addition, mp3 files are created automatically. These wav and mp3 files are stored in a mass storage system with a current total storage capacity of 60 TB. Mirroring of the wav files onto AIT cassettes and a hard disk RAID ensure data back up.

The complete data are thus exported to a system that will permit migration to future media and/or formats simply and without great expense.

Digitization not only ensures the preservation of these media, but also has advantages for users: digitized media can quickly be retrieved at computer terminals at the click of a mouse.

At www.mediathek.at, audio clips can be retrieved from the on-line catalogue. Alternatively, access is possible via the acoustic galleries that are arranged thematically and which offer media clips and background information.

FrG